GUIDE TO ADVERTISING AND SALES PROMOTION LAW

GUIDE TO ADVERTISING AND SALES PROMOTION LAW

Sallie Spilsbury

Cavendish
Publishing
Limited

London • Sydney

First published in 1998 by Cavendish Publishing Limited, The Glass House, Wharton Street, London WC1X 9PX, United Kingdom.

Telephone: 44 (0) 171 278 8000   Facsimile: 44 (0) 171 278 8080

E-mail: info@cavendishpublishing.com

Visit our Home Page on http://www.cavendishpublishing.com

Spilsbury, Sallie

Guide to Advertising and Sales Promotion Law

1. Advertising – Law and legislation – Great Britain 2. Sales Promotion – Law and legislation – Great Britain

I. Title

343.4'1'082

ISBN 1 85942 387 0

Printed and bound in Great Britain by
Biddles Ltd, Guildford and King's Lynn

This book is dedicated to the memory of Mary Fullard

PREFACE

The inspiration for this book was a guide to advertising law which was written by my former employer, the law firm Richards Butler, for its media and advertising law clients. That guide was widely complimented by those who received it and revealed a gap in the market for a concise guide to advertising and marketing law which could be of use to lawyers in private practice, to in house lawyers and to marketing and advertising professionals. This book is an attempt to plug that gap.

I would like to thank everyone who has helped to produce this book and who has offered encouragement and support. This includes my colleagues at the law firm Addleshaw Booth & Co, my former colleagues at Richards Butler and my friends and family. Thanks too to the regulatory bodies who have given consent to the reproduction of industry codes and guidelines.

I have attempted to state the law as at 1 June 1998.

Sallie Spilsbury
June 1998

ACKNOWLEDGMENTS

Extracts from the British Codes of Advertising and Sales Promotion and Committee of Advertising Practice Help Notes appear with kind permission of the Committee of Advertising Practice. Extracts from decisions of the Advertising Standards Authority appear with kind permission of the ASA.

Extracts from the Independent Television Commission Codes of Advertising Standards and Practice and Programme Sponsorship appear with kind permission of the ITC.

Extracts from Broadcast Advertising Clearance Centre guidelines appear with kind permission of BACC.

Extracts from the Radio Authority Advertising and Sponsorship Code appear with kind permission of the Radio Authority.

Extracts from the Independent Committee for the Supervision of Standards of Telephone Information Services Code of Practice appear with kind permission of ICSTIS.

CONTENTS

Contents

Contents

TABLE OF CASES

TABLE OF STATUTES

TABLE OF EUROPEAN LEGISLATION

PART ONE

LEGAL ISSUES

CHAPTER 1

REGISTERED TRADE MARKS

The function of trade marks

For a lawyer, the primary function of a trade mark is to indicate the origin of a product or service (the so called 'badge of origin' function). Trade marks can be thought of as identification symbols. As part of this function, trade marks serve to distinguish the goods or services of one business from those of other businesses.

Trade marks can be registered at the Trade Mark Registry, which operates a public register, or they can be unregistered. Registered trade marks are easier to protect and to enforce than their unregistered counterparts. They also tend to be more valuable. This chapter concerns registered trade marks and all subsequent references to trade marks in this chapter are references to registered marks. The protection of unregistered trade marks is considered in Chapter 2.

The law relating to trade marks is principally regulated by Act of Parliament. The relevant Act is the Trade Marks Act 1994 (the Act).

Why are trade marks important?

It is beyond dispute that brands and brand values should be safeguarded from plagiarists to preserve both their value and reputation in the marketplace.

From the point of view of a brand owner, a registered trade mark gives the owner the exclusive right to use the mark or to permit others to do so in the territory in which it is registered. A trade mark is attractive because it offers a *monopoly* in the use of the brand (at least in relation to the goods or services for which it is registered, and sometimes in relation to similar goods or services). This monopoly can last indefinitely, provided the trade mark is used more or less continuously as a brand name and renewal fees are paid to the Trade Mark Registry. A business's name and its brands are invariably among its most important assets. The relatively small outlay in applying for registration of valuable brands as trade marks can be invaluable in the long term, in order to preserve both the distinctiveness of the brands and the associated goodwill. The rights which a registered trade mark gives to the trade mark owner are far broader than those associated with an unregistered mark.

To quote from a recent case, *Mercury Communications Limited v Mercury Interactive (UK) Limited* (1995) FSR 850 (Laddie J):

If a trader wishes to bring passing off proceedings [to enforce an unregistered mark] he has to prove the existence of a reputation in his mark with potential customers. In the majority of cases this means that his common law rights will wither and disappear unless he continues to market and advertise his goods under the mark. Furthermore his rights are only breached if there is, or is likely to be, confusion in the marketplace which will cause him substantial damage. This should be contrasted with the rights acquired by a proprietor who registers a mark. His registration gives him a true monopoly. Subject to certain statutory defences the proprietor will be able to restrain any trader who uses the same or a sufficiently similar mark on the goods covered by the registration. This is so even if in the marketplace no confusion is being caused. Indeed he will be able to sue for infringement even if he is not using his own registered trade mark (subject to it being removed if prolonged non-use is proved). Furthermore with little effort any competently advised proprietor will be able to keep his registration in force indefinitely.

From the point of view of third parties, an appreciation of the breadth of the rights which a registered trade mark gives to its owner is important in order to avoid infringement. Trade marks may be unwittingly infringed. Innocence of the existence of a registration or a lack of intention to infringe is no defence to a claim for infringement.

The trade mark register

The UK trade mark register is divided into classes of goods and services. An application for registration has to stipulate the class or classes for which registration is sought. In addition, the application has to specify which particular goods and services within each class the application will relate to; for example, an application might be made in respect of insurance services in class 36 of the register. If the application is successful, the trade mark will be registered in respect of the classes and specifications contained in the application.

A registration will not necessarily give unrestricted monopoly rights to use the mark outside the goods and services for which it is registered.

Applying for a registration

Applying for a trade mark registration can be a complex matter. The advice of a solicitor or trade mark agent should be sought at an early stage. Applicants will need to make sure that the application is as exhaustive as it can properly be in terms of both the identification of the mark for which registration is sought and the classification and specification of goods and services. The Trade Mark Registry tend to be very helpful in relation to queries on the application procedure but they will not give legal advice to applicants.

The official fee for an application at the time of writing is £225 plus £50 for each extra class. Renewal fees (payable every 10 years) are currently £250 plus £200 for each extra class. If an application is opposed, the costs of pursuing the application will increase.

Conflicts with earlier registrations

Registration of a trade mark will not be permitted where an earlier registration exists on the register which is either:

(a) identical to the mark which is sought to be registered and registered in respect of identical goods or services; or

(b) identical or similar to the mark which is sought to be registered and registered in respect of identical or similar goods and services resulting in the likelihood of confusion on the part of the public; or

(c) identical with or similar to the mark which is sought to be registered and registered in respect of goods or services which are not similar where the earlier mark has a reputation in the UK and the use of the mark which is sought to be registered without due cause would take unfair advantage of or be detrimental to the distinctive character or repute of the earlier mark, unless the owner of the earlier mark consents to registration.

'Earlier registration' means not only a trade mark which is already registered or which has been applied for on the UK register, but also a registration having effect in the UK under the Madrid Protocol or as a Community Trade Mark. Both the Madrid Protocol and the Community Trade Mark are discussed below in relation to international trade mark registrations.

The reader will appreciate from the above that before applying for a trade mark registration, or choosing a new brand or product name with a view to making an application, appropriate searches should be made at the Trade Mark Registry, to check for existing registrations which might preclude registration. Such searches can be carried out quickly and inexpensively. Lawyers or trade mark agents can carry out the search or, alternatively, the register can be inspected in London, Manchester or Newport by any member of the public on payment of a fee.

What can be registered as a trade mark?

Any sign that is capable of graphic representation can be registered as a trade mark provided that it is capable of distinguishing the goods or services of the applicant from those of other undertakings.

This means that descriptive terms or words are difficult to register because they lack the necessary distinctiveness; for example, 'Clean Bright' for a floor cleaner will be difficult to register because it will be an uphill struggle to convince the Registry that the name is distinctive of a particular manufacturer. When selecting a brand, a name or a design it should be borne in mind that material which is not in everyday usage – for example, made-up words or everyday words which are used in an unusual sense – are likely to be easier to register because they are more distinctive. The public are not so likely to have to be educated by expensive promotional campaigns before they realise that such marks are associated with the applicant.

We shall consider each of these requirements in more detail.

A trade mark can be any sign capable of graphic representation

Sign should be interpreted broadly. It can be anything which conveys information; for example, in theory, a drawing of an electric shaver which appears on product packaging could be registrable, provided that it is sufficiently distinctive. What is important is that the sign is capable of being represented on paper. It is irrelevant that the sign is not normally depicted on paper; for example, sounds can be registered, provided that they can be represented on paper, say by musical notation.

What types of signs can be registered?

(a) *Words*, including personal and business names, slogans, straplines, letters and signatures.

(b) *Designs,* for example, logos, character designs and stylised words.

(c) *Internet domain names* are registrable, although the generic parts of domain names, for example, '.com', are regarded as non-distinctive. It is the remainder of the domain name (usually the beginning) which will be relevant for the purpose of assessing distinctiveness.

(d) *The shape* (including the three dimensional shape) *and appearance of packaging* can be registered: for example, the Coca Cola bottle and the Jif lemon juice container. Shapes which result from the nature of the goods themselves, which are necessary to give a technical result or which give substantial value to goods cannot be registered, however distinctive.

(e) *The likeness of individuals* (but see Chapter 10 for an analysis of the difficulties in securing such a registration).

(f) *Distinctive non-static sequences* which feature in a brand's advertising: for example, the well known Asda back pocket pat.

(g) *Jingles.*

(h) *Smells.*

(i) *Colours and combinations of colours* (provided they are sufficiently distinctive).

All in all the range of material that is capable of registration is much broader than brand names or business names, although it is those areas with which the majority of registrations are concerned.

Signs must be capable of distinguishing goods or services

The requirement that marks must be capable of distinguishing goods and services means in practice that the mark must denote the trader's goods and services and none other.

There is no automatic requirement that marks have to have acquired distinctiveness before they can be registered. What is important is that they are *capable* of fulfilling that function.

In some instances the Trade Mark Registry will require evidence of distinctiveness to be produced before a mark can be registered. Marks devoid of any inherently distinctive character, for example, those of a purely descriptive nature, will generally not be registrable unless it can be shown to the satisfaction of the Registry that the marks have acquired distinctiveness through use. The mere fact that the mark has been used, even over a long period of time, is unlikely, in itself, to prove 'distinctiveness' to the satisfaction of the Registry without accompanying evidence of brand awareness.

A recent High Court decision[1] concerning the registrability of the word Treat as a trade mark for a toffee flavoured spread emphasised the descriptive nature of such a mark and held that:

> It must be shown in a case of this sort that the mark has really become accepted by a substantial majority of persons as a trade mark – is or is almost a household word.

Evidence will be required to show acceptance by the 'substantial majority'. This term is as yet undefined, but would seem to suggest that the trade mark must be accepted as a badge of origin by well over 50% of the population if a trade mark registration for a descriptive term is to be achieved. Marketing professionals will appreciate the difficulties of establishing such a level of brand awareness.

If we return to the Clean Bright example for floor cleaner, in view of the descriptive nature of the name, the applicant is likely to be asked to provide evidence of distinctiveness to show that a substantial majority of the public associate the name and product with the applicant to the exclusion of other manufacturers of similar products.

---

1 *British Sugar plc v James Robertson & Sons* [1996] RPC 281.

Prohibited signs

UK and/or European law prohibits the registration of certain marks without consent, as follows:

(a) the royal arms and royal flags;

(b) words, etc, suggestive of royal patronage or authorisation;

(c) the Union Flag and the UK national flags, where the mark misleads or is offensive;

(d) the national flags and emblems of certain other countries and international organisations;

(e) other arms granted by the Crown;

(f) the Olympic symbol.

Trade marks will also not be registered if they are contrary to public policy or accepted principles of morality, likely to deceive the public or prohibited by UK or European Community law.

The requirement for good faith

An application to register a trade mark can be refused if it is not made in good faith. If there is no intention to use the mark in relation to the goods or services for which the application is made at the time of application, it will be vulnerable to refusal on this ground. Similarly, an application which is made with the intention of holding a third party to ransom, for example, with the intention of preventing someone with a genuine claim to the mark from registering it, will be liable to refusal.

The international registration of trade marks

A registration on the UK register will be of effect in the UK only. If registration is sought in other territories, separate applications should be made to the appropriate national authorities. There are, two systems which facilitate the international registration of trade marks.

(a) The Community Trade Mark (CTM) applies throughout the European Union. If a CTM is obtained, it gives one registration for the whole of the European Union. So, for example, the owner of a CTM which it uses in the UK could in theory sue for infringement of the mark if it is used without permission in Spain or any other EU Member State. The CTM is a relatively new creation and it is still too early to assess accurately how it will work in practice. Applications to register CTMs have far exceeded expectation.

(b) The Madrid Protocol. This allows a number of national registrations to be made by way of a single application to a central body, the World Intellectual Property Organisation which is based in Geneva. In contrast to the CTM, the Protocol is merely a facilitator to the grant of a number of national registrations rather than one supranational registration.

Can a registered trade mark be removed from the trade mark register?

A trade mark can be revoked in limited circumstances. These are as follows:

(a) Where the registered mark is not used for five years following registration or where use of the trade mark is suspended for a continuous period of five years.

(b) Where the application to register was made in bad faith, usually where the applicant has no intention to use it or where false or misleading evidence was filed to support the application.

(c) Where the trade mark loses its distinctiveness after registration *and* where this is due to either the acts of or the inactivity of the trade mark owner, or where, as a result of the use of the mark by the proprietor or with its consent, the mark is liable to mislead the public.

This last circumstance covers the situation where a mark ceases to become a badge of origin, that is, an identification label for a particular manufacturer, and instead becomes a generic name. To put it differently, the mark becomes a noun rather than a brand. This is what happened to the marks Hoover, Biro and Aspirin, to give just a few examples. They have all passed into everyday usage as generic terms.

In order for a registration to be revoked on the ground that it has become generic, there has to be fault on the part of the trade mark owner in allowing the situation to exist. This can either take the form of the owner itself using its brand as the name of a type of goods rather than its own particular goods, or where the owner has stood back and allowed others to use it generically. In order to avoid an application for revocation, care must therefore be taken to police a registered trade mark to ensure that its distinctiveness is maintained and its use sustained.

Trade marks which are devoid of any distinctive character or which were registered in bad faith can also be declared invalid, as can trade marks which fall under the heading of prohibited signs (see above) or whose shape should not properly have been registrable, for example, because it results from the nature of the goods themselves.

A mark will be removed automatically from the register where renewal fees are not paid (renewal fees are payable every 10 years), although there are provisions for late payment.

What is an infringement of a registered trade mark?

The owner of a trade mark has exclusive rights in the trade mark, which are infringed by the use of the trade mark without his consent.

What amounts to use for the purposes of infringement?

Use has to be in the course of trade to constitute an infringement. Trade is defined to include any business or profession.

Use includes oral or aural use, for example, in a voice-over or the reproduction of a jingle, as well as written or graphic use.

The Act refers to use as being, in particular:

(a) affixing the sign to goods or packaging;

(b) offering goods for sale or offering or supplying services under the sign;

(c) importing or exporting goods under the sign;

(d) using the sign in business papers or advertising.

Those involved in the *preparation of* infringing material will be treated as infringers if they know or have reason to believe that the use of the mark is not authorised by the mark's owner.

This part of the Act was designed to clarify the position of entities involved in the preparation of infringing material who do not have responsibility for its content. It is uncertain, but, it is submitted, doubtful, that it will apply to protect advertising agencies who are not on notice of the potential infringement, unless the agency has no responsibility for the content of the artwork or the copy. It may, however, apply to printers who simply produce copies of infringing advertisements, at least until they are put on notice of the infringement.

Owners of marks which are being infringed might find it worthwhile putting all parties involved in the infringement on notice of the infringement. Such a step might act as an effective deterrent. Once those parties without responsibility for the infringing material are on notice, repetition of the infringement may render them liable.

Publishers, the providers of billboard space or broadcasters which provide the media on which advertisements appear may be infringing a trade mark if they continue to offer the means for publication of an advertisement having been put on notice of the infringement.

Those with responsibility for content will be liable without being put on notice.

What amounts to infringement?

The following unauthorised acts amount to infringement:

(a) use of a sign which is *identical* to the trade mark in relation to goods and services which are *identical* with those for which it is registered (s 10(1) of the Act);

(b) use of a sign which is *identical* to the trade mark in relation to goods and services which are *similar* to those for which it is registered so that there is a likelihood of confusion or association on the part of the public (s 10(2) of the Act);

(c) use of a sign which is *similar* to the trade mark in relation to goods and services which are *identical* or *similar* to those for which it is registered so that there is a likelihood of confusion or association on the part of the public (s 10(2) of the Act);

(d) use of a sign which is *identical* or *similar to* the trade mark in relation to goods or services which are *not similar* to the goods and services for which it is registered where the mark has a reputation in the UK and the use of the sign being without due cause takes unfair advantage of or is detrimental to the distinctive character or the repute of the trade mark (s 10(3) of the Act).

What do the above provisions mean in practice?

Identical marks used in relation to identical goods

Where the infringement takes the form of the use of a mark which is identical to the registration in respect of identical goods or services, there is no necessity to demonstrate that the use of the infringing mark is likely to cause confusion in the minds of the public.

What is meant by identical marks?

There has been no judicial guidance about what is meant by identical marks. Often it will be self-evident. It is open to argument whether minimal differences between marks will disqualify marks from being regarded as identical. Take an example: DIRECT LINE is a trade mark belonging to Direct Line Insurance plc. Use by a third party of DIRECT-LINE or DIRECTLINE, although not strictly the same, would, it is suggested, be regarded as identical.

It is also likely that the use of a trade mark by a third party as a domain name which entails a slight variation, for example, the use of directline.com, would be considered to be use of an identical mark.

What is meant by identical products?

It was held in *British Sugar v James Robertson* (1996) FSR 281 that the specification of goods or services for which registration has been obtained should be construed strictly. In that case, British Sugar produced a syrup topping for desserts called 'Silver Spoon Treat'. The word 'Treat' was registered for dessert sauces and syrups. James Robertson produced a toffee flavoured spread which was sold as 'Robertson's Toffee Treat'. British Sugar commenced legal proceedings for infringement of their Treat trade mark. The court had to decide whether dessert sauces and syrups were the same as toffee spread for the purposes of s 10(1). It was held that:

> ... when it comes to construing a word used in a trade mark specification, one is concerned with how the product is, as a practical matter, regarded for the purposes of the trade ... The Robertson product is not, for the purpose of the trade, a dessert sauce.

The goods were therefore not identical for the purposes of s 10(1).

Identical or similar marks in relation to identical or similar goods or services

In order to establish infringement under s 10(2) of the Act, the circumstances of use must be such that there is a likelihood of confusion or association in the minds of the public.

What is meant by similarity between marks?

Determining whether there is similarity between marks is a matter of art rather than science.

The comparison is mark for mark. External circumstances, for example, the fact that the genuine brand is known only to be sold in exclusive department stores and the infringing goods are available in corner shops, are irrelevant to the issue of likelihood of confusion and should be ignored for these purposes. The likelihood of the public misremembering the mark so that it is only imperfectly recollected should also be kept in mind.

When considering whether two marks are similar, regard should be had to the way they sound as well as the way they look.

Example

Wagamama Limited v City Centre Restaurants plc [1995] FSR 713

The plaintiff operated a restaurant under the name Wagamama. It also owned a number of trade marks in the word Wagamama registered in respect of restaurant services. The defendant opened a chain of restaurants which it initially called Rajamama. That name was subsequently changed to Raja Mama's following the plaintiff's initial letter of complaint that the Rajamama name infringed its trade mark.

The court was asked to consider whether the name Raja Mama's was an infringement of the plaintiff's Wagamama trade mark. There was no argument as to whether the marks were used in relation to identical goods and services. The questions were whether the two marks were similar and whether there was a likelihood of confusion or association.

In assessing the similarity of the two marks, the court had regard to the phonetic impact of the two marks as well as the visual similarity. The court accepted that when seen side by side the marks were easily distinguishable but noted that that was not in itself determinative of the issue of whether there was similarity, if the marks sounded alike.

Additionally, the court stressed that it should be borne in mind that customers often have an imperfect recollection of how marks look and sound. They do not often have the luxury of being able to compare marks side by side. The public are more likely to take with them the overall impact of a mark as opposed to a detailed recollection of its component parts. So the overall or principal impact of the mark is at least as important as a literal examination of its constituent parts.

In *Wagamama*, the fact that the Wagamama mark was on its face meaningless was held to make imperfect recollection by the public more likely. The court also observed that the fact that both businesses offered relatively inexpensive restaurant services made imperfect recollection more likely. Presumably, the more expensive and/or exclusive the business in question, the less allowance will be made for imperfect recollection on the ground that the customer would be expected to remember the brand name of an expensive item but less likely to recall the brand name of an inexpensive item or an everyday purchase.

What is meant by similarity of goods and services?

Useful guidance is set out in the *British Sugar* case. That case sets out the factors to take into account in deciding whether a mark is used in relation to similar products or services for which it is registered. The factors to take into account are as follows:

(a) The respective uses of the goods or services.

(b) The respective users of the goods or services.

(c) The physical nature of the goods or acts of service.

(d) The respective trade channels through which the goods or services reach the market.

(e) In the case of self-service consumer items, where in practice they are respectively found or are likely to be found in supermarkets and in particular whether on the same or different shelves.

(f) The extent to which respective goods or services are competitive. This inquiry may take into account how the trade classifies goods, for example, whether market research companies put the goods or services in the same or different market sectors.

What is meant by the likelihood of confusion to include likelihood of association?

Straightforward confusion about the source or origin of goods or services will be sufficient to establish infringement, for example, where A's goods are mistaken for B's goods – B being the owner of the trade mark.

If the similarity in the marks is such that it leads to the impression that the businesses of A and B are connected, for example, that the trade mark owner has expanded its range to include the defendant's goods or that the owner has licensed the defendant to produce goods under the trade mark, that will also be sufficient to establish infringement.

When the Act came into force on 31 October 1994, it was widely believed that it extended the concept of association beyond the narrow interpretation set out above. It was thought that the Act might extend the rights of trade mark owners so that a trade mark could be infringed if it was only brought to mind by the use of a third party of a similar mark, even though there was no confusion about origin. Some commentators thought that circumstances where a trade mark was simply called into mind without any confusion could result in an infringement.

The point was argued in the *Wagamama* case. Wagamama argued that the fact that the public would think of their mark when they saw the Rajamama mark was sufficient to give rise to an infringement even if no one was actually confused into believing that the businesses were the same or connected.

The court held that there had to be confusion about the origin of goods or services before there could be an infringement under s 10(2) of the Act. Confusion could take two forms. It could be confusion in the straightforward sense, that is, where the public confuse the goods or services on offer as coming from the same source. It could also be in the association sense, that is, that the sources of the goods or services are connected, such as by a licence agreement. In *Wagamama*, the court held that there was a likelihood of this type of confusion. It went on to observe that the mere fact that the use of a mark might remind the public of the trade mark owner's mark would *not* be sufficient to give rise to a trade mark infringement.

The part of the judgment that referred to the need for confusion about origin was *obiter*. This means that it was in fact an observation on this aspect of the law but that it was not part of the crux of the court's decision. As such, it is not binding on other courts, which may come to a different conclusion if asked to consider the same issue. The *Wagamama* judgment is, however, carefully considered and it is submitted that it offers a sound basis for advertisers to interpret the law pending a decision on the point from a higher court.

Identical or similar marks in relation to non-similar goods and services

The above can be an infringement where the trade mark:

(a) has a reputation in the UK

(b) and the use of the sign being without due cause

(c) takes unfair advantage of or is detrimental to the distinctive character or the repute of the trade mark

(d) for example, by causing confusion (see below).

Little guidance is given in the Act as to the meaning of the above concepts.

Is there a need for confusion?

Section 10(3) does not actually refer to the need to show confusion in order to establish infringement. However, in recent judgments the court has indicated that it will be necessary to find some confusion, or the likelihood of it, before a finding of infringement under s 10(3) can be made; for example, *BASF plc v CEP (UK) plc* (Unreported, 26 October 1995).[2] The rationale for this decision is that neither the distinctive character nor the repute of the mark can be adversely affected when there is no risk of confusion. Section 10(3) can therefore be reformulated for the purposes of providing a working rule of thumb. It can be said that it applies to the use of signs which are identical or similar to the trade mark in relation to goods and services which are not similar to the mark where the use causes a likelihood of confusion on the part of the public.

As with a s 10(2) infringement, confusion can be confusion as to origin or confusion in the association sense, that is, that the trade mark owner has extended its range of products or has licensed the user of the mark to make use of it.

---

2   See, also, *Baywatch Productions Co Inc v Home Video Channel* [1997] FSR 22.

Does the infringing use have to be use in the trade mark sense, that is, as a badge of origin, or can any type of use of the trade mark infringe?

Trade marks serve to distinguish goods and services as originating from a particular source.

If a third party uses a trade mark in a way that does not serve to distinguish its goods and services from those of others, but rather in a descriptive way or as an indication of the quality of the goods and services, will that be an infringement?

In the *British Sugar* case, Robertson introduced a toffee spread which they called Robertson's Toffee Treat. British Sugar alleged trade mark infringement. Robertson argued that they were not using Treat in a trade mark sense, that is, as a badge of origin. Instead, their use of the word 'Treat' was descriptive. As such, they argued the use could not be an infringement.

The judge held that there was no overriding requirement that there had to be trade mark use before a trade mark could be infringed. It is therefore theoretically possible that a purely descriptive use can infringe.

Example

Renault is a registered trade mark belonging to Regie Nationale des Usines Renault. Can company X, a spare parts manufacturer, advertise its products as 'spare parts for Renault vehicles' without infringing the Renault registration? The use of the Renault mark does not imply that the parts originated from Renault. The use of the trade mark is not therefore in the badge of origin sense.

Section 11(2) of the Act provides that a registered trade mark is not infringed by:

(a) the use by a person of his own name or address;

(b) the use of indications concerning the kind, quality, quantity, intended purpose, value, geographical origin, the time of production of goods or of rendering of services, or other characteristics of goods or services; or

(c) the use of the trade mark where it is necessary to indicate the intended purpose of a product or service (in particular as accessories or spare parts);

provided the use is in accordance with honest practices in industrial or commercial matters.

In the Renault example, a mere reference to the Renault trade mark would not be an infringement. Use of the mark is necessary to indicate the intended purpose of the spare parts as parts for Renault vehicles.

If the use of the trade mark was dishonest, it might well be an infringement. If, for example, the advertisement featured the Renault logo as its most prominent feature, or otherwise led the public to assume that the parts in question were actually manufactured by Renault, such use would be unlikely to be in accordance with honest practices and would therefore be an infringement.

On the facts of the *British Sugar* case, the judge found that there was no infringement on the ground that Robertson's products were not similar to British Sugar's products (see above, p 14, in relation to infringement). Additionally, the judge found that even if there had been an infringement, Robertson's use would have fallen within s 11(2) of the Act, that is, it was a permissive descriptive use of the word 'treat'.

The court laid down guidance for the interpretation of s 11(2) as follows. The purpose of a trade mark is to indicate origin. In determining whether a use falls within s 11(2) one should:

(a) look at the whole context of use;

(b) distinguish between uses of the mark;

(c) decide whether the defendant is using the sign descriptively or as a trade mark to indicate the origin of the goods. If it is to indicate the origin of the goods, a s 11(2) defence will *not* be available. If the use is descriptive, the defence will be available, provided that the use is in accordance with honest practices in industrial or commercial matters.

Can a trade mark be used to identify goods and services as belonging to the trade mark owner?

Section 10 (6) of the Act makes it clear that the infringement provisions which are set out in s 10 do not prevent the use of a trade mark by any person for the purpose of identifying goods or services as those of the proprietor.

There is a proviso, however. Any use of a trade mark for the purpose of identifying goods and services as those of the proprietor which is otherwise than in accordance with honest practices in industrial and commercial matters shall be treated as infringing the trade mark if the use without due cause takes unfair advantage of or is detrimental to the distinctive character or repute of the trade mark.

The most obvious impact of the section, and its main objective, is in relation to *comparative advertising*. This is where a competitor's trade mark is used to identify the goods or services that are being compared to the advertised goods. There is no intention of confusing the public about the origin of the competitor's products in such advertising.

The legal issues surrounding comparative advertising generally are explained in Chapter 8. This chapter contains a detailed analysis of the recent case law on trade mark infringements in relation to comparative advertising. The cases contain important guidance for advertisers in this field.

Under the pre-1994 law, it was an infringement to use a competitor's trade mark in the course of comparative advertising. The position has now been changed, thanks to s 10(6).

What are the requirements of s 10(6)?

Section 10(6) states that a trade mark will not be infringed if it is used to identify goods or services as those of the trade mark owner or its licensee. However, where that use is not in accordance with honest practices in industrial or commercial matters, such use *will* infringe the mark where, without due cause, it takes unfair advantage of, or is detrimental to, the distinctive character or repute of the mark. There has been a flurry of cases concerning the interpretation of the section. In the main, the cases have been surprisingly favourable to advertisers. The leading case is *Barclays Bank plc v RBS Advanta* [1996] RPC 307. It is worth considering the case in detail, as it has important implications for advertising law generally, outside the issue of comparisons.

The facts

Barclays Bank plc (Barclays) is the owner of the trade mark Barclaycard in respect of credit card services.

RBS Advanta (RBS) was launching a new credit card. To test the market it sent out pilot samples of its proposed advertising literature. Barclays objected to the literature complaining that it infringed their Barclaycard trade mark. The literature took the form of three documents: a letter, a leaflet and a brochure all of which formed part of a single mail shot. Barclays' complaint concerned the leaflet and brochure read together.

The leaflet

The leaflet was headed '15 ways the RBS Advanta card is a better card all round'.

It then listed 15 favourable points about the RBS card: for example, no annual fee; the RBS card was accepted wherever the Visa sign was displayed; and free travel insurance. The leaflet made no reference to Barclays or Barclaycard. In particular, it did not feature the Barclaycard registered trade mark.

The brochure

The brochure included a table comparing a number of features of the RBS Advanta card with those of other major credit cards, including the Barclaycard standard Visa. The brochure featured the Barclaycard trade mark.

The complaint

Barclays argued that the use of the Barclaycard trade mark in the brochure when read in conjunction with the leaflet was not in accordance with honest practices in commercial matters. It was therefore an infringement of its trade mark in accordance with s 10(6) of the Act.

No complaint was made about the content of the brochure other than the fact that it featured the trade mark. In particular it was accepted that the content of the comparative table was correct.

Barclays argued that it was the content of the leaflet that was dishonest. It was dishonest in two ways as, follows:

(a) It did not compare like with like. In particular, the literature made no mention of certain ancillary benefits offered to Barclaycard holders but not available to RBS Advanta cardholders. RBS's leaflet emphasised the lower interest rate available to their cardholders. This was misleading and dishonest because RBS did not also point out the other advantages of using Barclaycard.

(b) Of the 15 points mentioned in the leaflet, seven were also shared by Barclaycard, for example, both cards were accepted wherever the Visa symbol was displayed. It was not therefore true to say that the RBS card was better than the Barclaycard in all of the 15 ways shown.

Both of these arguments were unsuccessful.

The judgment

The judge confirmed that the purpose of s 10(6) was to allow comparative advertising so long as the use of a competitor's trade mark is honest.

The judge sanctioned Barclays' approach that the literature should be read together, that is, that the leaflet was to be read together with the brochure. He observed that if advertising documents are intended to be or are likely to be read together, then the advertisement should be considered as a whole. An illegitimate use of a trade mark will not be saved from a finding of infringement by the expedient of putting the trade mark on one document and the dishonest information on the other. The same principle is likely to apply to other areas of law.

The judge considered the proviso to s 10(6). The proviso states that any use of a trade mark for the purpose of identifying goods and services as those of the proprietor which is otherwise than in accordance with honest practices in industrial or commercial matters shall be treated as infringing the trade mark if the use without due cause takes unfair advantage of, or is detrimental to, the distinctive character or repute of the trade mark.

The judge observed that the test as to whether comparative advertising is in accordance with honest practices is an objective one. If the use of the trade mark is considered dishonest by members of a reasonable audience, for example, if it is significantly misleading, it will infringe. The subjective intention of the advertisers is not the determining factor.

The codes of practice in relation to advertising, for example, the CAP codes or other industry codes, are not the gauge by which to measure honesty. Advertisements can breach those codes but still be honest, and vice versa.

The nature of the goods and services which are being advertised is relevant. What is tolerable in advertisements for second hand cars may not be thought honest by reasonable people for advertisements for medicines.

The fact that the advertising pokes fun at the competitor's product or emphasises the benefits of the advertiser's products without pointing out the advantages of those of the trade mark owner is what is to be expected of comparative advertising and is not of itself dishonest.

The judge chose not to make a literal, word for word analysis of the content of the leaflet. Instead, he adopted a more broad brush approach, by considering the advertisement as a whole in recognition of the way the majority of the public would consider an advertisement. He observed that it was well recognised that advertising copy is considered by the public as hyperbole. The use of such puffery does not in itself make advertising dishonest. The more specific a statement, the more likely it is to be taken seriously; the more general, the less so. On the facts, the judge found that the advertisements considered as a whole conveyed the message that the RBS card offered an overall better deal. It was unlikely that the reasonable reader would be misled into thinking that all 15 points in the leaflet were only available to RBS Advanta card holders.

The final section to the proviso to s 10(6), which reads: 'If the use without due cause takes unfair advantage of or is detrimental to the distinctive character or repute of the trade mark', adds nothing of significance to the section, save to emphasise that the harm caused to the trade mark by the comparative advertising must be more than minimal or trivial.

The approach set out in the *Barclays* case has been endorsed in subsequent cases.

Vodafone Group plc v Orange Personal Communications Limited [1997] FSR 34

The case concerned an advertising campaign mounted by Orange which compared its operating tariff with those of certain of its competitors including Vodafone. The advertising included the phrase: 'On average Orange users save £20 every month.' The saving was expressed to be a comparison with Vodafone's and Cellnet's equivalent tariffs. Vodafone sued Orange over the use of the comparison alleging malicious falsehood (see Chapter 3 for details of this cause of action) and infringement of its registered trade mark for the word Vodafone.

Endorsing the *Barclays* judgment, the judge observed as follows:

> This is a case about advertising. The public are used to the ways of advertisers and expect a certain amount of hyperbole. In particular the public are used to advertisers claiming the good points of a product and ignoring the others ... and the public are reasonably used to comparisons – knocking copy as it is called in the advertising world. This is important in considering what the ordinary meaning may be. The test is whether the ordinary man would take the claim being made as one made seriously. The more precise the claim, the more it is likely to be so taken – the more general or fuzzy, the less so.

In interpreting the advertisement, the judge thought the public would understand it to mean that if Orange users had been on Vodafone or Cellnet, making the same use as they did on Orange, they would, as a mathematical average, have had to pay £20 more a month. He held that the advertisement would not be understood to mean that, if Vodafone users transferred to Orange, £20 per month would automatically be saved.

Taken objectively, the phrase was not dishonest and the advertisement did not infringe Vodafone's trade mark.

British Telecommunications plc v AT&T Communications (UK) Limited [1997] 5 EIPR D-134

The BT trade mark was used in an advertisement by AT&T in which it was stated that on the whole, AT&T's international dialling rates were cheaper than BT's. In particular, it stated that when a particular plan operated by AT&T was used for a chosen country, AT&T was up to 40% cheaper than BT for international calls. BT sued for trade mark infringement, alleging that the claim relating to the up to 40% saving was dishonest.

The judge endorsed the *Barclays v Avanta* approach and held that each advertisement must be considered as a whole and that a minute textual examination of the advertisement was not something on which a reasonable reader would normally embark. He held that the advertisement taken as a whole would be understood to be promising substantial savings on AT&T's customers' bills. He did not think that the advertisement would be understood as asserting a saving of up to 40% and acknowledged that there would be a serious question to be tried on the honesty of the advertisement if it were so understood.

The topic of comparative advertising is considered further, in relation to legal issues generally, in Chapter 8.

The approach adopted by the court is realistic in that it seeks to interpret advertisements in the same way as the general public interpret them. The approach tends to differ from that adopted by the regulatory authorities such as the Advertising Standards Authority. It is in that arena where the real restrictions on comparisons show their teeth. Often a disgruntled competitor unhappy about a comparison will find it more productive to complain under the codes rather than to sue for trade mark infringement, or to pursue one of the other substantive legal remedies available to it.

Misuse of a well known mark

Particularly well known trade marks, whether registered as trade marks in the UK or not, are protected from infringement by s 56 of the Act which provides as follows:

> The proprietor of a trade mark which is entitled to protection under the Paris Convention as a well known trade mark is entitled to restrain by injunction the use in the UK of a trade mark which is identical or similar to his mark in relation to identical or similar goods and services where the use is likely to cause confusion.

The Act provides no assistance in defining a well known trade mark. The Paris Convention referred to is the Paris Convention for the Protection of Industrial Property 1883. That Convention is similarly unhelpful in explaining what is meant by a well known mark. The best advice is: where you know that you are dealing with a notorious trade mark with a high public recognition factor, for example, Coca Cola, be wary of using a mark which is identical to or similar to the trade mark for the same or similar goods and services.

The right under s 56 is independent of any UK trade mark registration. Even if a search of the trade mark register does not reveal a registration, s 56 can be relevant. It is not necessary for the owner of the well known mark to trade in the UK or to have a trading reputation in the jurisdiction, but the mark must be well known in the UK.

How to avoid infringement

(a) Carry out searches at the Trade Mark Registry to determine whether your advertising, branding and other promotional material will infringe a registered trade mark. Searches are relatively inexpensive and quick to carry out. Your solicitor or trade mark agent will be able to carry out the search for you. Alternatively, anyone can visit the registry in London, Manchester or Newport to carry out the search for a small fee.

(b) Trade marks are territorial rights. Searches should therefore be carried out in each territory where the advertising will appear to ensure that it does not infringe in those territories. Your lawyer, trade mark agent or the Trade Mark Registry can help you to carry out the searches.

(c) If a registered mark appears on the register which is the same as the mark you want to use or similar to it, take legal advice about what you can do.

(d) If you wish to use a well known mark in your advertising take advice, even if it does not appear to be registered as a trade mark.

(e) If you want to use a trade mark in a descriptive way, for example, to describe the characteristics of a product such as spare parts, you can do so, but you should make sure that the advertisement is not misleading: for example, that it does not make false statements or imply that the product originates from the owner of the trade mark. If in doubt take legal advice.

(f) If you wish to use a trade mark in a comparative advertisement, you can do so, but the advertisement must not mislead. If in doubt take legal advice.

(g) Remember that the trade mark registration can give the owner wider protection than the goods or services for which it is registered.

Trade marks and the internet

Use of a third party's trade mark on the internet carries with it the potential risk of infringement proceedings. The internet is global. In contrast, trade mark systems tend to be territorial. A registration in the USA will not permit its owner to sue if the trade mark is infringed in the UK because the US mark is irrelevant to the UK (unless the Paris Convention famous mark provisions come into play – see above, p 22). It is therefore not unusual for the same mark to be owned by different, and unconnected, entities in different countries. Acts of infringement will fall to be judged at the place where infringement occurred. Typically, this will be where the advertising material is read. This can have disastrous consequences.

Imagine that company A has a trade mark registered in the UK in respect of greeting cards. It places an advertisement on the internet which is intended to be aimed at the European market, A having no intention of trading elsewhere.

Company B also has a trade mark registration for the same mark in the USA for greeting cards. It downloads company A's advertisement in the USA. Company A then receives a writ from company B claiming infringement of its trade mark under US law.

As yet, there is no UK case law to indicate how the UK courts would treat such a situation. It is suggested that if the company which is advertising has no intention to trade in other jurisdictions, for example, if company A had no intention of doing business in the USA, the mere fact that a third party's US trade mark appears in its advertising ought not to constitute trade mark infringement.

In order to protect it as far as possible, an advertiser should put a disclaimer on its internet advertising making it clear in which territories it is seeking to advertise or to do business. There is no guarantee that a disclaimer will be sufficient to avoid liability at the end of the day, but it would be sensible to do all that is possible to minimise the risk until the law in this area is settled.

If company A had intended to advertise and to trade in the USA, under US law its advertisement would almost certainly have been an infringement of company B's mark.

The position is similar under UK law. It has recently been held that a German company could be sued in England in relation to the promotion of its services to persons in England on, amongst other things, an internet web site, even though the advertisement in question was placed in Germany.[3]

It is also advisable for the advertiser to seek its own trade mark registrations in the territories in which it is advertising. This will protect it from infringement proceedings in those territories and will give it a base for the protection of its mark from infringers overseas.

Criminal offences

The Act creates a number of criminal offences of trade mark infringement in relation to goods (but *not* services).

The use without consent of an identical mark, or of a mark which is likely to be mistaken for a registered mark, in the course of a business, amounts to an offence if the defendant does not have a reasonable belief that the use of the sign was not infringing the trade mark. The detailed provisions of the Act can be summarised as follows.

A person commits an offence who, with a view to gain for himself or another, or with intent to cause loss to another, and without the proprietor's consent:

(a) applies to goods or their packaging a sign identical to or likely to be mistaken for a registered trade mark;

(b) sells, hires, offers for sale or hire, or distributes goods which bear such a sign;

(c) has in his possession, custody or control in the course of a business any such goods with a view to their being sold, hired, offered or distributed;

(d) applies a sign identical to or likely to be mistaken for a registered trade mark to material intended to be used for labelling or packaging goods, as business paper in relation to goods, or for advertising goods;

(e) uses, in the course of a business, material bearing such a sign for labelling or packaging goods, as business paper in relation to goods, or for advertising goods; or

(f) has in his possession custody or control in the course of a business any such material with a view to the doing of anything by himself or another which would be an offence under paragraph (e) above.[4]

---

[3]   *Mecklermedia Corporation and Another v DC Congress GmbH* (1997) *The Times*, 27 March.

[4]   Trade Marks Act 1994, s 92.

Similar provisions exist making it an offence to make an article specifically designed for making copies of a sign identical to or likely to be mistaken for a registered trade mark knowing that the article is to be used in producing, packaging or labelling goods.

No offence is committed in relation to the above unless the trade mark in question has a reputation in the UK and the use of a sign takes unfair advantage of or is detrimental to the distinctive character or the repute of the trade mark. An offence can only be committed in relation to any act done after the registration has been published in the official journal of the Trade Mark Registry, the *Trade Mark Journal*.

Penalties

On summary conviction, imprisonment for up to six months, or a fine up to the statutory maximum (currently £5,000), or both.

On conviction in the Crown Court, an unlimited fine, or imprisonment of up to 10 years, or both.

Orders for the forfeiture of infringing goods can also be made.

The provisions are enforced by trading standards departments. Private prosecutions can, and are, brought by trade mark owners and/or trade associations.

® and ™ symbols

When a trade mark is registered, the ® symbol can be used in conjunction with the trade mark to enforce the message that rights are claimed in the mark and that they will be enforced. If the mark is not registered, it is a criminal offence to use the ® symbol. The symbol ™ may, however, be used for both registered and unregistered marks.

The use of crests in advertising

It is fairly common for direct mailings to feature a crest or a coat of arms. There is a danger in using such designs without taking legal advice. The use of the royal arms, or arms which closely resemble the royal arms, is a criminal offence under s 99 of the Act. Similarly, the use of a device, emblem or title in such a way as is likely to lead to the belief that the advertiser or promoter supplies goods or services to the royal family, or any member of that family, is also a criminal offence under the same section of the Act. The reader is also referred to Chapter 5 for details of potential liability under the Trade Descriptions Act 1968.

CHAPTER 2

PASSING OFF

The law of passing off gives a plaintiff the right to protect its goodwill (meaning its business reputation) from misappropriation by a third party. Putting it more simply, the law will give X the means to stop Y trading on the back of X's name and reputation.

There is no monopoly in an unregistered trade mark

Passing off does not offer automatic protection for brands, distinctive designs or other marks from misappropriation. If a trader wishes to ensure that competitors cannot use its marks, it should register them as trade marks. Unregistered brand names or get up can be used simultaneously by separate traders for the same goods or services except to the extent that the use constitutes a passing off. Actions for passing off are often expensive and difficult to win. In order to maximise protection for trade marks, they should be registered wherever possible.

An overview of the law of passing off

It is outside the remit of this book to examine the evidential difficulties which exist for a plaintiff who wishes to establish that passing off has occurred. Suffice to say that the difficulties are often significant. Legal advice should be taken before a claim in passing off is made or threatened.

The elements that must be shown to establish passing off were set out in the case of *Erven Warwink BV v Townend and Sons Limited* (the *Advocaat* case) [1979] AC 731 as follows:

(a) a misrepresentation

(b) made by a trader in the course of trade

(c) to prospective or ultimate customers

(d) which is likely to injure the business or goodwill of another trader and

(e) which causes actual damage to a business or goodwill of the trader by whom the legal action is brought or will probably do so.

These elements were reformulated in a useful way in the case of *Reckitt and Colman Products Limited v Borden Inc* (the *Jif lemon juice* case) [1990] 1 WLR 491 as follows:

(a) The plaintiff must establish a *goodwill or reputation* attached to the goods or services which he supplies. The goodwill should be present in the mind of the public to an extent that the identifying get up (whether it consists simply of a brand name or a trade description or the individual features of labelling or packaging), under which the plaintiff's particular goods or services are offered to the public, is recognised by the public as distinctive of the plaintiff's goods or services.

(b) There must be a *misrepresentation* by the defendant to the public which leads or is likely to lead them to believe that goods or services offered by him are the goods or services of the plaintiff or are associated with the plaintiff.

(c) There must be *damage* suffered, or likely to be suffered, by reason of the erroneous belief engendered by the defendant's misrepresentation. The damage is likely to be evidenced by confusion on the part of the public. The confusion should be shown to affect a substantial number of members of the public.

Reverse passing off

Reverse passing off occurs where the defendant's misrepresentation is not that the goods and services are those of the plaintiff, but rather where the misrepresentation is that the plaintiff's goods are those of the defendant.

We now examine the requirements necessary to establish passing off in more detail.

Goodwill or reputation

The plaintiff must establish a goodwill or reputation in his/her goods or services. Strictly, the reputation is not in the brand name or get up itself, but rather it is in the plaintiff's goods or services. These goods/services are recognised as the plaintiff's products by virtue of the plaintiff's distinctive trading features.

What is goodwill?

Goodwill is a difficult concept to define. It is essentially the benefit that a good name and reputation brings with it. It has been defined as 'the attractive force which brings in custom. It is the one thing which distinguishes an old-established business from a new one'.[1]

Goodwill does not exist independently of trade. A business which has not traded will have no goodwill and will not therefore be in a position to bring a successful claim for passing off.

---

[1]   *IRC v Muller* [1901] AC 217

Goodwill is territorial. In order to establish passing off in the jurisdiction of the English court, the plaintiff must show that it has acquired goodwill in its goods or services in the jurisdiction. In the case of foreign complainants there must be some business in the jurisdiction either directly or through an intermediary such as an agent. It is not, however, necessary for the foreign plaintiff to have a place of business in the UK, provided that there are customers in the jurisdiction.

A company will not acquire goodwill if it is simply advertising, unless trade is about to commence imminently. Even then, it is a moot point whether advertising alone can generate protectable goodwill in a business. It is suggested that, as a matter of logic, a pre-launch advertising campaign ought to be capable of creating protectable goodwill, although this point is yet to be tested in the courts.

Goodwill can be limited within the jurisdiction. If goods/services are only available in a particular area, the goodwill will be limited to that area where the goods/services are known.

Goodwill can continue to subsist even though the business to which it attaches has ceased to trade. A defunct business can therefore bring an action for passing off.

Goodwill requires distinctive marks

In order for goodwill to be acquired by a business, the brand name or get up (meaning the external appearance of goods in the form in which they are seen before purchase) of the goods or services must be a sufficiently distinctive badge of origin so that the public, on seeing or hearing the brand, etc, will associate the goods or services with the business and with none other.

The subject of distinctiveness and badges of origin are considered above, in Chapter 1.

Generally, the more descriptive the brand name, the harder it will be to show that it is distinctive of a particular business and therefore the harder it will be to establish goodwill.

Example

An office cleaning business called Office Cleaning Services sought to stop a rival business from calling itself Office Cleaning Association on the ground that the choice of such a similar name was a passing off. The court refused to make such an order on the basis that office cleaning was a descriptive term. It noted that where a trader adopts for its trade name words that are in common use, confusion was likely to follow (*Office Cleaning Services Limited v Westminster and General Cleaners Limited* [1946] RPC 39).

The less distinctive a mark is, the less likely that relatively small differences in trading style will amount to a passing off. To hold otherwise would be to grant a trader an unfair monopoly in commonly used words.

Notwithstanding the above, commonly used words can in some circumstances become distinctive of a particular trader when they are used in conjunction with a distinctive logo or get up or are written in a particular style. In such circumstances it is unlikely that the words taken alone will be sufficiently distinctive to generate goodwill in the goods or services unless they are accompanied by the distinctive get up, logo or stylisation.

A common get up or word can, over time, usually as a result of extensive marketing campaigns, become distinctive of a business. For example the Jif lemon juice container, which is a yellow plastic lemon-shaped container containing lemon juice, has been held to be distinctive of its manufacturer despite the fact that there is nothing inherently distinctive in the shape of a lemon to indicate that the lemon juice was the product of that particular manufacturer. The manufacturer of Jif lemon juice was able to stop a rival company from selling lemon juice in similar containers on the ground that such action amounted to a passing off. Evidence was produced to show that the container had come to be associated by the public with the manufacturer. Despite the generic nature of its shape it had become distinctive of the plaintiff's goods. This acquisition of distinctiveness in commonplace names and objects is sometimes called a *secondary meaning*.

What kinds of marks can be distinctive?

The following marks are in theory capable of being distinctive, taken together or possibly in isolation:

(a) brand names – including personal names;

(b) the design of packaging – that is, part of the get up;

(c) the shape of packaging – that is, part of the get up;

(d) the size of packaging – that is, part of the get up;

(e) logos;

(f) slogans;

(g) jingles;

(h) general advertising style;

(i) titles;

(j) the appearance of business premises;

(k) labels;

(l) pictures;

(m) colours;

(n) signatures;

(o) stylised words and letters;

(p) the combination of commonplace features in a distinctive way, for example, the layout of the front page of a magazine or an advertisement.

Can the appearance, shape or functional qualities of the goods be distinctive?

The appearance or functional features of goods (as opposed to their packaging) will generally not be capable of protection in passing off.

The importance of such features is usually not the fact that they indicate the origin of the products, but rather their aesthetic or functional worth. Passing off will not protect the plaintiff who can show that its goods are widely recognised if he cannot also show that the goods are recognised and associated with him. The plaintiff must show that the defendant is misrepresenting those elements which serve to distinguish the plaintiff's goods in the mind of the public from those of other traders.

In the case of *Bostick Limited v Sellotape GB* [1994] RPC 556, the plaintiff alleged passing off by the defendant because the defendant brought out a similar product to the plaintiff's Blu-Tack product. In particular the plaintiff claimed that the fact that the defendant's product was the same colour as Blu-Tack (blue) was a deceptive misrepresentation. The court rejected the plaintiff's complaint. The colour of the defendant's product could not be seen until it was removed from the packet. The misrepresentation was not operative at the point of purchase. The packaging of the defendant's product was clearly distinguished from the plaintiff's product, as was its name (Sello Tak).

The misrepresentation

The misrepresentation can be express or implied. It must deceive the public in some way, whether intentionally or otherwise.

(a) The simplest form of misrepresentation is the straightforward representation that the defendant's goods or services are those of the plaintiff when they are not, for example, the market store trader selling counterfeit clothing featuring the distinctive marks of a well known fashion house.

(b) Alternatively, the making of untrue representations about the nature of goods rather than their origin can be a passing off, for example, if a trader represents the plaintiff's rejected stock as being the plaintiff's approved stock.

(c) Any false representation that the goods or services are approved by or connected with the plaintiff in some way can be a passing off. For example, where advertising inserts were put into a newspaper without the newspaper's consent it was found that this constituted a misrepresentation that the inserts were connected with or associated with the newspaper. The defendant's conduct amounted to a passing off.

In the case of *United Biscuits (UK) Limited v Asda Stores Limited* [1997] RPC 513, United Biscuits, who manufacture the Penguin biscuit, commenced proceedings against Asda in respect of their 'own brand' chocolate biscuit called Puffin. Asda were found to be passing off. The misrepresentation by the sellers of Puffin biscuits was held to be that the Puffin packaging would cause a substantial number of members of the public to suppose that Puffin biscuits were made by the same manufacturers as Penguin biscuits. It was accepted that the public would not be confused into thinking that the Puffin biscuit was the same as the Penguin biscuit. The erroneous belief that the biscuits came from the same source was sufficient to render the packaging a passing off.

For a passing off claim to succeed, the connection between the plaintiff and the defendant which is being misrepresented must be such that it would lead the public to accept the defendant's goods or services on the faith of the apparent connection with the plaintiff.

(d) A false representation that the defendant's business is connected with the plaintiff's business, for example, that they are sister companies, can be a passing off, as can the representation that the businesses are one and the same, for example, where the defendant's business answers the telephone in the name of the plaintiff's business.

Misrepresenting goods or services as belonging to a particular class

Misrepresentations that goods or services are of a particular type, originate from a particular area or belong to a particular class can be a passing off where the classes of goods enjoy a distinctive reputation.

Examples

It has been held that the use of the name 'Champagne' amounts to a passing off when used in relation to wines which do not originate from the Champagne region of France. It has also been held that the name Advocaat cannot be used for any drink which is not made in accordance with the traditional recipe for Advocaat.

Recently, Cadbury Schweppes was restrained by manufacturers of Swiss chocolate and the Swiss chocolate trade association, Chocosuisse, from calling one of its products 'Swiss Chalet' on the ground that Swiss chocolate has a distinctive reputation in Britain. It was held that the public would be confused into thinking that Cadbury's product was Swiss chocolate when it was not.[2]

---

2 *Chocosuisse Union des Fabricants Suisses de Chocolat v Cadbury* (1997) *The Times*, 25 November.

Innocent misrepresentations

A misrepresentation does not have to be deliberate or fraudulent to give rise to passing off. A misrepresentation which is made innocently without an intention to deceive the public can still give rise to liability. It is the effect of the misrepresentation that is important rather than the motivation of the maker. The plaintiff must, however, be able to show at least the probability of deception caused by the misrepresentation. In practice the court is more likely to find that there is a likelihood of deception where there is evidence of, or at least an inference of, the defendant's intention to pass off.

In the *United Biscuits* Penguin/Puffin case, one of the factors drawn to the court's attention was a written design brief which Asda prepared for its product designers. The brief stated that the Asda biscuit should have 'brand beater' characteristics, one of the design objectives being that it should clearly match against the Penguin brand using cues such as colour and typography. The judge in the case referred to the brief in his judgment as evidencing a conscious decision on the part of Asda to 'live dangerously'. Whether the judge was correct in taking the document into account is a moot point. The fact is that he did take it into account and was to some extent swayed by it. The moral is to ensure that all documents surrounding product development and marketing are carefully worded to ensure that if litigation ever arises, there is nothing in them which could give rise to the inference that there was an intention to pass off, or an appreciation of the legal risks being run but a decision taken to ignore them.

Likely to injure the plaintiff's business or goodwill

Injury to goodwill is invariably caused as a result of confusion in the mind of the public arising from the misrepresentation. The damage caused must be, or must be likely to be, more than minimal.

The case law differs as to what type of damage is sufficient to give rise to passing off. The general principles can be formulated relatively simply but case law throws up exceptions, which make it difficult to set out the law definitively.

It seems clear that damage to a business's *general reputation* is insufficient. What must be shown is damage to *goodwill* (or business reputation).

Example

Harrods Limited, the company which runs Harrods department store, brought an action in passing off against a business which proposed to run a preparatory school under the name The Harrodian School. The action failed. One of the grounds was that the plaintiffs were unable to show the likelihood of any damage to its goodwill. The court considered what would happen if the school became enmeshed in a scandal of some type. Whilst the attendant publicity might temporarily tarnish Harrods' good name generally, the court held that there was no real danger that customers of Harrods would withdraw their custom from the store. The publicity would not, therefore, affect the plaintiff's goodwill associated with running a store. The court considered that damage to reputation without corresponding damage to the goodwill of the business would not be sufficient to give rise to an action in passing off.

It should, however, be noted that there was a powerful dissenting judgment disagreeing with the majority in the Court of Appeal. The dissenting judgment only serves to demonstrate the subtle difficulties involved in grappling with the concept of goodwill (*Harrods Limited v Harrodian School Limited* [1996] RPC 697).

Types of damage arising from misrepresentations

The most common type of damage to goodwill arising from a misrepresentation is loss of revenue caused by the diversion of the plaintiff's business to the defendant.

A second type of damage relates to loss of economic opportunities, for example, the loss of opportunities to license marks into different market sectors or to franchise.

There is also a less obvious, and more insidious, type of damage. The inability of the plaintiff to exercise control over the content or quality of the goods or services offered by the defendant constitutes a real risk of injury to goodwill. If the defendants offer, or are likely to offer, a lesser standard of product than the plaintiff's product, then those customers who do business with the defendant believing it to be, or to be associated with, the plaintiff will also believe that the inferior goods or services are connected with the plaintiff.

A further insidious type of damage is caused by the defendant being in a position to strengthen its position in the marketplace as a competitor of the plaintiff by taking the benefit of the plaintiff's reputation.

Some cases indicate that a fifth type of damage is the erosion of the distinctiveness of the plaintiff's brand, get up, etc, caused by the misrepresentations of, and the use by, the defendant. Clearly the use by a third party of the plaintiff's marks will erode the exclusive association with the plaintiff.

Different areas of business

Passing off can occur where there is no overlap in the businesses of the plaintiff and defendant, that is, where they are not direct trade rivals.

This area of the law of passing off comes very close to protecting the plaintiff's marks themselves rather than the goodwill in the corresponding goods or services. Some of the cases in this area appear to extend the traditional functions of passing off to quasi-registered trade mark law. The recent *Harrods* case indicates a more restrictive approach is being taken by the Court of Appeal and it is suggested that plaintiffs may find it increasingly difficult to bring a successful passing off claim where the parties trade in different areas of business.

In those cases which have been successful, the court has found that the plaintiff's mark is so well known, and so associated with the plaintiff, that the use of it in a different business context will give rise to an representation that the plaintiff has diversified its business activities.

Example

The makers of the well known plastic Lego toys successfully restrained a third party from using the Lego mark on plastic garden irrigation equipment on the basis that the public might be deceived into thinking that the plaintiff had expanded its business into garden equipment or had licensed the use of its Lego mark on the defendant's goods. The court accepted submissions that the Lego mark had become part of the English language in the sense that everyone associated the Lego mark with the Lego company. The court recognised that, where the plaintiff's mark was not so well known, it would be more difficult for the plaintiff to establish that it would be understood as denoting the plaintiff's products in different business areas.

In the *Lego* case, it was found that confusion would be likely to cause damage to the plaintiff, notwithstanding that the parties did not share a common field of activity. The decision is not as clear as it might be on this aspect but it would seem that the court was influenced by the fact that Lego gave evidence that they might in the long term future expand into the defendant's line of business. Lego might have been deprived of its long term licensing and franchising opportunities as a result of the defendants' activities (*Lego System Aktieselskab v Lego M Lemelstrich* [1983] FSR 155).

Some difficulties which the plaintiff might encounter in establishing passing off where the defendant is in a different area of business are as follows:

(a) Passing off does not protect marks as such. It protects goodwill in goods or services. The plaintiff must show that it is the goodwill that is damaged by the use of its mark. Damage to general reputation is not sufficient to establish passing off. The court observed in the *Harrods* case that the Harrods mark might be universally recognised, but that the business with which the public associate it was not all-embracing. The court went on to say that to be known to everyone is not to be known for everything. This statement is difficult to reconcile with the Lego decision but, as suggested above, it seems to be indicative of a more restrictive judicial approach.

(b) The type of connection which is misrepresented should be such that it would lead the public to suppose that the plaintiff is responsible for or connected with the defendant's goods or services.

(c) Deception will be difficult to establish where the fields of activity of the parties are far apart. The further removed the respective areas of business, the less likely that any member of the public could reasonably be confused into thinking that the businesses are connected.

Avoiding passing off in advertising and promotions

(a) Avoid the adoption of advertising styles, product get up, brand names or other marks which are confusingly similar to those of third parties

(b) Bear in mind that a representation which implies *any type* of connection with a third party can be a passing off. The law protects against a wider range of statements than the straightforward representation that X's product is manufactured by Y.

(c) The reaction of the public to advertising and promotional material should be assessed in a realistic manner. Shoppers are often in a hurry. They will not analyse material to the *n*th degree before purchasing goods, especially low cost consumer items. If the immediate and overall effect of advertising, get up or promotions would be likely to cause confusion, then placing disclaimers in small print, for example, 'this product has no connection with ...' is unlikely to avoid liability.

(d) Care should be taken in relation to material which features a competitor's mark to ensure that the material will not confuse the public, who may look at the material in a hurried way, into believing that there is a connection between the advertiser/promoter and the other business which is referred to.

Example 1

Comparative advertising

As we have seen, passing off does not give a brand owner the exclusive right to its brand name, get up or other marks. It restricts use of those marks only to the extent that the use is deceptive. Advertising which makes use of a competitor's marks by way of comparison is therefore permissible to the extent that it is not deceptively confusing. This can be a fine line to draw. An example where the advertiser got it wrong is the case of *McDonald's Hamburgers v Burger King (UK)* [1987] FSR 112. The case concerned an advertisement by Burger King featuring a photograph of the Burger King

Whopper Burger above the strapline 'IT'S NOT JUST BIG, MAC'. The Big Mac is, of course, McDonald's well known equivalent product to the Whopper Burger.

McDonald's alleged that the advertisement was a passing off. They said that the advertisement misrepresented that the Burger King product was associated with the McDonald's product. The claim was successful. The advertisement was found to be a passing off. The advertisement failed to differentiate the competing products or to make it clear that it was comparing the products.

All comparative advertisements carry the risk that that the advertisement will amount to a passing off if care is not taken to make it unambiguously clear that there is no connection between the products being compared.

Example 2

Promotions

In the case of *Kimberley-Clark Limited v Fort Sterling Limited* [1997] FSR 877, the defendant, trading as Nouvelle, devised packaging for its toilet tissue which featured a promotional flash in the following terms: 'Softness guaranteed (or we'll exchange it for Andrex).' In smaller lettering the packaging stated that Andrex was a registered trade mark belonging to Kimberley-Clark Limited and that Andrex was a competitor's brand which did not belong to Nouvelle.

Despite these sensible precautions for avoiding confusion, the court found that the packaging was a passing off. Andrex was the premier brand in the market for toilet tissue. Nouvelle had only a tiny share of the market in comparison. To the majority of the public, Nouvelle was an unfamiliar mark. Customers were unlikely to scrutinise the packaging to the extent that they would notice the disclaimers. They were likely to see the Andrex mark and to associate the product with Andrex.

This case illustrates how difficult it can be to make use of a competitor's marks in advertising or promotions without committing a passing off.

(e) A misrepresentation may be unintentional. On the other hand, where there is evidence to indicate that there was an intention to imitate the plaintiff's advertising or get up or to otherwise pass off goods or services that will tell against the defendant. Care should therefore be taken to avoid the impression that there was a decision to 'live dangerously'. Briefs to advertising agencies, etc, should not be capable of being misconstrued.

(f) As the *Andrex* case demonstrates, where there has been a long use by the third party of a distinctive get up or brand there will be a special obligation on the competitor to avoid confusion or deception.

(g) Take care with statements that competing products are interchangeable or similar when they are not. Such statements may not clearly be understood to distinguish the products and could be a passing off.

(h) Remember that the public may imperfectly recollect a business's marks, especially in the case of low value consumer products. You can unintentionally pass yourself off as a business by the use of a similar mark to that of the plaintiff which, whilst not identical to the plaintiff's mark, would cause confusion amongst the public.

CHAPTER 3

DEFAMATION, TRADE LIBEL AND MALICIOUS FALSEHOOD

INTRODUCTION

This chapter is concerned with a practical guide to the substantive law relating to defamation, malicious falsehood and trade libel. The subject of the remedies which are available to plaintiffs in defamation actions are considered in Chapter 14.

DEFAMATION

Damage to reputation

The law of defamation operates to protect the *reputation* of a business or an individual from the making of false and defamatory statements. Damage to reputation is a necessary prerequisite to a claim in defamation. The law of defamation does not offer redress against statements which are untrue, unless the statements cause damage to reputation or standing.

Example

To say that company X's product does not taste good will not affect X's reputation, although it might affect its profits. There can be no action for defamation in respect of such a statement, although there may be an action for trade libel (see below, p 52).

To say that company X's product is dangerous, because vital health and safety precautions are not taken during the manufacturing process, will not only damage X's profits but also its reputation as a responsible manufacturer. Such a statement might also damage the reputation of X's directors and employees with responsibility for complying with the regulations. It carries with it the implication that they are carrying out their duties negligently or incompetently. Company X and its directors and employees might be able to sue for defamation in respect of the damage to their respective reputations if they can show that the statement would be understood to refer to them.

Reputation is not restricted to a person's business reputation or to their moral reputation. It extends to all aspects of a person's standing in the community. To portray a person as a figure of fun can be defamatory because it lowers that person's general standing in the community.

In the case of *Dunlop Rubber Co Limited v Dunlop* [1921] 1 AC 367, the plaintiff was the inventor of a pneumatic tyre. He assigned his interest in the invention to Dunlop Rubber Company along with the right to use his signature and likeness as a trade mark. The defendant embarked on an advertising campaign containing pictures which were recognisably of the plaintiff, which depicted the plaintiff as a fop. It was held that such a representation was capable of being defamatory because it exposed the plaintiff to ridicule.

What is a defamatory statement?

A defamatory statement is therefore a statement which causes damage to reputation or standing.

There is no uniformly accepted definition of what constitutes a defamatory statement. The definitions that do exist are somewhat outdated. They are as follows:

(a) Would the words used tend to lower the plaintiff in the estimation of right thinking members of society generally? If so, they will be defamatory.

(b) A statement concerning any person which exposes him to hatred, ridicule or contempt is defamatory.

(c) A statement which causes any person to be shunned or avoided is defamatory.

(d) A statement which has a tendency to injure any person in his office, profession or trade is defamatory.

(e) A false statement about a man to his discredit is defamatory.

It is important to note that it is the *tendency* of the statement that is important and not its actual effect. There is no requirement that a plaintiff proves that the statement has damaged his reputation.

Whether a particular statement is defamatory will depend on the facts of that case and the context in which the material is published.

With the warning that it should not be relied on for definitive guidance, set out below is a sample of meanings which would probably be found to be defamatory.

(a) The accusation that someone has been dishonest or has otherwise acted fraudulently is almost always going to be defamatory.

(b) An allegation that disparages someone's performance in their trade or profession will generally be defamatory.

(c) The accusation that someone has broken the law will generally be defamatory.

(d) The accusation of racism will also probably be defamatory.

(e) Allegations about child abuse will almost always be defamatory, but query other types of sexual conduct. Would it make ordinary people think less of a person if he or she were exposed as having an adulterous affair? What if the affair was with someone of the same sex? To expose someone as a transvestite has been held to be defamatory, but query whether a different jury might come to the opposite decision.

(f) To refer to someone as having certain medical conditions might be defamatory. In a recent case it was held that to portray someone as having an eating disorder was defamatory. Query whether it would be defamatory to say that someone is HIV positive or that they have AIDS.

(g) To query someone's mental stability or health will probably be defamatory.

(h) To represent that a business or person cannot pay its debts or is insolvent or bankrupt will generally be defamatory.

Some of the difficulties in determining whether a statement is defamatory are illustrated by the above. To decide whether a statement is defamatory one first has to determine what a statement means. This is often a difficult task.

The meaning of the statement

Often, the same statement will be capable of interpretation in a number of ways. It is quite usual in defamation actions for one party to assert that a statement means one thing and for the other party to assert an alternative meaning. Often both meanings are equally credible.

For example, consider the following statement: 'Confectioner X has today been charged with an offence under The Food Safety Act.' Is the correct construction the literal meaning of the statement, that is, the mere fact of a charge? Or does the statement have a less obvious, but more serious meaning, namely that X has been negligent in complying with hygiene standards? Or does it mean that X is suspected of wrongdoing, but may not have actually done anything wrong?

The questions are rhetorical! The test is what would the reasonable audience interpret the statement to mean.

The need to consider all possible meanings

Because of the risk that statements could mean more than one thing to different people, when checking copy for potential defamatory statements, care should be taken to assess all possible meanings which the material might bear. *The fact that a particular meaning was never intended will not provide a defence to a defamation claim.*

In determining meaning, those involved in clearing advertising and promotional material should take into account that the reasonable audience is accustomed to the ways of advertisers and will expect a certain amount of hyperbole which they would probably discount when interpreting a statement. However, the temptation to rely on a subjective interpretation of a statement should be avoided. The test is what would the reasonable audience take this statement to mean, rather than what do we (the makers of the statement) mean. To clear a statement on that basis that no one will take it seriously is potentially a very dangerous course.

Quite often, a statement on its face may not have a defamatory meaning but there will be a secondary meaning which may not be readily apparent. This secondary meaning is known as *innuendo.* In order to appreciate the innuendo, it will generally be necessary for a reader or viewer to have knowledge of extraneous facts which are not apparent from the material. The plaintiff can sue for defamation in respect of the innuendo if only a tiny minority of the audience knows of the extraneous facts. It is irrelevant whether the person with responsibility for the publication knows of the extraneous facts. A good example, which demonstrates the operation of innuendo in the field of the use of personalities in advertising, is the case of *Tolley v Fry* [1931] AC 333.

The facts

The defendants, Fry, were manufacturers of chocolate. They placed an advertisement for their chocolate in a number of newspapers. The advertisement featured a caricature recognisably of the plaintiff, Mr Tolley, who was a well known amateur golfer. Mr Tolley's name also appeared in the advertisement. The caricature featured the plaintiff wearing his golfing clothes with a bar of the defendant's product sticking out of his pocket. The whole item was clearly an advertisement. On its face it contained nothing likely to lower Mr Tolley's reputation amongst right thinking members of society generally.

The defendant alleged an innuendo meaning based on the fact that he was known to be an amateur golfer. There was no reference to his amateur status in the advertisement. The case was in 1931, a time when the concept of amateur would clearly have been understood to mean that the sports person in question made no financial gain from his or her sporting activities. Mr Tolley argued that the advertisement meant that he had permitted his likeness to be used in an advertisement for gain and reward. As such, readers of the advertisement, with knowledge of his amateur status, would think that he had prostituted his reputation as an amateur golfer and was, therefore, guilty of conduct unworthy of his amateur status. Those persons aware of Mr Tolley's amateur status, he argued, would understand this innuendo meaning.

The court accepted Mr Tolley's interpretation of the meaning of the article and the fact that it was defamatory of him. The court observed that the expectation would be that no reputable firm would have the effrontery and bad taste to take the name of a person for its advertising without permission and the use of Mr Tolley's name and likeness implied that he had lent himself willingly to the scheme. The court considered this allegation to be most offensive.

Those involved in the clearance of material should therefore be wary of 'hidden' innuendo meanings.

What is a statement?

Statements need not be in verbal. Cartoons and drawings can be defamatory, either taken alone or in conjunction with captions and text. Television and film footage can also be defamatory.

The term statement is used throughout this chapter as a term of convenience.

A guide to spotting defamatory statements

It is dangerous to rely on the types of statements which have been judged to be defamatory in the past as reliable guides to whether a particular statement will be defamatory. It is for that reason that the warning which prefaces the list on pp 40–41 appears. Whether a statement is defamatory is a question which is, to a large extent, dependent on the context in which particular assertions are made and the reaction of the ordinary people at the time of publication to the words. What was thought to be defamatory to right thinking members of society 50 years ago might not be thought so today, and vice versa.

Another element of uncertainty in defamation actions is that the meaning to be attributed to a statement is determined by a jury (subject to certain exceptions) who also decide whether the statement is defamatory. Whilst the jury is perceived to be a bulwark for the preservation of free speech there is no doubt that in practical terms it introduces a real element of uncertainty into this area of law. In deciding whether a statement is defamatory, allowance must always be made for the wildcard element because of the inherent unpredictability of the jury.

Statements of fact can be defamatory, as can expressions of opinion or comment. Liability will not necessarily be escaped by couching defamatory statements as matters of opinion or as comment. The defences available for factual statements are, however, different to those available for comments/opinion (see below, p 46).

The whole of the publication in question, whether it be a newspaper article, an advertisement, a television programme, etc, must be considered when deciding whether a statement is defamatory. The headline, captions, script and text must be considered together in conjunction with any accompanying pictures or photographs.

In the case of *Charleston v News Group Newspapers Limited* [1995] 2 AC 65, a newspaper reported that a computer game used the faces of well known actors in conjunction with the bodies of porn actors. It published photographs of the actors superimposed on the bodies of people engaged in indecent acts. The pictures and headline to the article gave the impression that the actors *had* consented to the use of their images in the computer game, when in fact they had not. The plaintiffs sued for defamation in respect of the misleading nature of the picture and headline. The rest of the article, however, made it clear that the actors had not consented to the use of their images in the computer game. The article as a whole was not misleading, although the pictures and headline taken in isolation were. It was held that the headline and photographs must be read with the full article and therefore the plaintiffs could not rely on the defamatory meaning conveyed to readers who only looked at parts of the article. The material must be read as a whole.

This is not a rule that is set in stone. In certain cases, it may be reasonable for a reader to only look at part of the material, for example, a front page splash on a newspaper is likely to be construed in isolation if the body of the material is contained elsewhere.

The question which those engaged in the clearance of advertisements should ask is would the *reasonable reader or viewer* think less of the complainant as a result of the statement? The test here is objective. It is tempting to consider the question subjectively, that is, 'do I think this is defamatory?', but this is a misguided approach. The statement should be considered in the context of society's attitudes generally. The intentions of the maker of the statement are irrelevant in determining both meaning and the question of whether a statement is defamatory.

Liability will not be escaped by putting forward the defamatory allegation as rumour or supposition rather than a matter of fact or personal opinion.

Identification

It does not matter whether a plaintiff is referred to by name in the statement. The test is whether the words would reasonably be understood to refer to that person. It is irrelevant whether the maker of the statement intended the words to refer to that individual or even that he did not know that the plaintiff exists.

Classes of people

Large and indiscriminate classes of people cannot be defamed, for example, the statement that the advertising industry is full of lazy and incompetent people would not give any particular member of the industry the right to sue for defamation even though the statement is undoubtedly defamatory. Such a statement could not reasonably be understood to refer to a particular person or persons.

However, to say that all the account handlers in the XYZ agency are lazy and incompetent could be defamatory of each of the particular account handlers, provided the number of account handlers was reasonably limited. If the XYZ agency was an international conglomerate the class might still be too wide for any one individual to say that the words could be understood to refer to him.

Key terms: libel and slander

Libel

A libel is a defamatory statement in a permanent form in respect of which there is no defence. Defences are dealt with below, p 46. The expression 'permanent form' includes radio, television and cable broadcasts and theatre performances. If a person sues for libel there is no requirement that he or she proves actual loss suffered as a result of the libel. Damage is presumed.

Slander

A slander is a defamatory statement in a non-permanent form, typically a statement that is spoken, but not recorded, in respect of which there is no defence. If a person sues for slander he or she will generally have to prove actual damage suffered as a result of the statement. The exception to the need to prove actual damage is in relation to certain classes of slander, the most relevant of which are imputations that a person has committed a criminal offence and imputations that disparage a person in his trade, business or profession. Where the exceptions apply, damage will be presumed and need not be proved.

Action for defamation – the burden of proof is a real difficulty

A person wishing to sue over a defamatory statement has very little to prove. He must show only the following:

(a) that the words complained of are defamatory;

(b) that the words refer to him; and

(c) that the words have been published to a third party. Publication is a wider concept than the activities of a commercial publisher or broadcaster. A statement which is made to a single third party will constitute publication. Publication can take place by e-mail and over the internet.

If the action is for slander and does not fall within the special categories referred to above, the plaintiff must also prove damage suffered as a result of the statement. The plaintiff's burden is therefore fairly light.

Crucially, the statement which the plaintiff complains about will be presumed to be false. To put it differently, the plaintiff will *not* have to prove the falsity of the statement.

The burden of proof then switches to the defendant. The defences are considered below. A defence will usually involve proving the truth of what has been said.

This operation of the burden of proof means that actions for defamation are very difficult to defend successfully.

Defences and tips on how to argue them successfully

Statements of fact – justification

It is a complete defence to prove that the substance of a statement of fact, or the gist of it, is true. The defence is known as *justification*.

The meaning which has to be justified is the meaning attributed to the statement by the court. The importance of being able to justify all potential meanings and inferences should not be overlooked. Claims can be made in respect of unintended meanings and innuendo meanings. In order to defend such claims successfully, the unintended meaning must be proved to be true.

Often *proving* the truth of a statement can be difficult. The proof must be in the form of admissible evidence. Mere supposition, rumour or evidence of a genuine belief that the evidence is true will not suffice. The repetition of defamatory statements which have been published elsewhere will not excuse a defendant from having to prove the truth of the statements.

If there is concern that a statement is defamatory, it is advisable to collect verifiable evidence to prove the truth of the statement before publication.

Evidence might consist of signed statements from individuals. It is not unusual for defences to collapse because the people who co-operated in supporting the statement are not willing to give evidence in court. The availability of signed statements before publication would go some way to overcoming such difficulties.

All documentary evidence to support statements should be retained.

Before making a plea of justification, the defendant should believe the words to be true and intend to prove their truth at trial. There should also be reasonable evidence available at that stage to support the plea, or there must be reasonable grounds to suppose that the evidence will come to light during the course of the proceedings. The defendant is entitled to take into account all sources which will become available to him during the litigation process, including evidence which the plaintiff may give during cross-examination or documents obtained during the discovery process.

Opinion or comment – fair comment on a matter of public interest

Where the defamatory statement is not a statement of fact but is a comment or an expression of opinion, the defence of fair comment will apply. In order to establish the fair comment defence, it must be shown that the comment or opinion is:

(a) based on facts, and that those facts are true (essentially the same criteria as justification); and

(b) honest; and

(c) on a matter of public interest.

The facts on which the comment is based do not have to be mentioned in full but it is advisable to make some mention of them alongside the comment or opinion, if only as a summary.

It must be clear that the comment or opinion *is* comment or opinion rather than an assertion of fact. The test as to what is opinion and what is fact is objective. The key question is, 'what would ordinary readers or viewers think?'

Care should be taken to ensure that comment or opinion would clearly be understood to be comment or opinion. The use of phrases such as 'it seems to me' or 'in our view' will help to establish this, although they will not be conclusive.

Honest comment

The question of whether comment is honest involves the following questions:

(a) Taken objectively, is the comment one that an honest minded person could have made on the facts which can be proved to be true? This is for the defendant to prove.

(b) If so, is the comment the defendant's honest opinion? It is for the plaintiff to prove that it is not.

Even if the comment taken objectively satisfies the first question, that is, it is an opinion which a reasonable person could have held on the facts, the plaintiff will succeed in his/her claim if he/she can show that the comment was not honest on a subjective level. If the comment was not made honestly it will be considered to have been actuated *by malice*.

'Malice' is a technical term which will arise again in relation to the other causes of action and defences considered in this chapter. It generally means dishonesty, for example, the publication of a comment that is not honestly held. If a defendant is reckless, that is, he does not consider or care whether what he publishes is true or false, a defendant will be treated as if he made the statement maliciously.

An example of the legal conception of malice

Horrocks v Lowe [1975] AC 135

Horrocks and Lowe were councillors representing opposing political parties. Mr Lowe verbally attacked Mr Horrocks at a council meeting alleging, amongst other things, that he had deliberately misled the council and political colleagues. Speeches at council meetings are protected by qualified privilege (see below, p 49), which is a type of defence which, like fair comment, can be defeated by malice. The question was whether Mr Lowe was acting maliciously when he made the comments in question. The court observed that Mr Lowe's political antagonism to Mr Horrocks had resulted in Mr Lowe having a state of mind of unreasoning prejudice against Mr Horrocks: such a state of mind amount to malice in the ordinary sense of the word, that is, spite or ill will. However, the legal meaning of malice is narrower. Because Mr Lowe genuinely believed the truth of his statements and his opinion was one which a reasonable person could have held, he was not found to have been malicious in law.

Public interest

This concept stretches beyond the public actions of public officials. The activities of private companies have been held to be in the public interest. By analogy, comments made as part of an advertising campaign or a sales promotion are likely in principle to be of public interest, although much will depend on the individual context.

Privilege

Certain classes of statement are privileged. The types of statement to which privilege of either type attaches are of little relevance to the law of advertising or sales promotion under the present law and as such a detailed consideration of them falls outside the remit of this book.

Statements can be subject to absolute privilege or qualified privilege. Absolute privilege is a complete defence to a claim for defamation. Statements made by MPs during parliamentary proceedings are covered by absolute privilege. Qualified privilege is a defence unless the plaintiff can show that the defendant published the statement maliciously (see above, p 48, for the definition of malice). Fair and accurate reports of judicial proceedings are covered by qualified privilege.

The right to reply to an attack

Where a person or a business's reputation is criticised in public, the subject of the criticism is entitled to exercise a right to reply in public by making a response which may include defamatory material, provided that the reply is not published maliciously, that it is proportionate and relevant to the original attack and that the publicity given to the reply is commensurate with the publicity given to the original attack.

Consent

If a person consents to the publication of a defamatory statement, the consent will operate as a defence if proceedings are commenced by that person for defamation. The consent must be consent to the actual defamatory statement that has been published. It will not be sufficient to say that X agreed to appear in an advertisement and therefore cannot sue for libel if he happens to be portrayed in a defamatory way in the advertisement. If X did not consent to the publication of the actual defamatory material which is published, the fact that he/she agreed to appear will not operate as a defence.

Denial of responsibility for publication or innocent dissemination

As a general rule, any person involved in the publication of defamatory material can be sued, ranging from the author to the newspaper vendor who sells copies of newspapers containing the defamatory material.

A person may therefore be involved in the publication of defamatory material even though he/she had no responsibility for its content. Section 1 of the Defamation Act 1996 provides a defence for parties who do not have primary responsibility for publication provided that:

(a) they took reasonable care in relation to the publication; and

(b) did not know or had no reason to believe that they had caused or contributed to the publication of a defamatory statement.

Primary responsibility

The defence is *not* available to the author, editor or commercial publisher of the statement complained of, or their employees or agents. Such people are assumed to have primary responsibility for content.

For the purposes of this defence:

(a) *Author* means the originator of the statement, but does not include a person who did not intend the statement to be published. If there was no intention for the statement to be published, an author can still rely on this defence.

(b) *Editor* means a person having editorial responsibility for the content of a statement or the decision to publish it.

(c) *Publisher* means a commercial publisher which issues the material to the public or a section of the public in the course of its business.

The defence will be available to people involved in the following activities, or activities which are analogous to them:

(a) printing;

(b) producing;

(c) distributing; or

(d) selling

the defamatory material.

Where the defamatory material is a film or sound recording, the defence will be available to those involved in:

(a) processing;

(b) making copies of;

(c) distributing;

(d) exhibiting; or

(e) selling

the defamatory material.

The broadcaster of a live programme will not have primary responsibility in respect of the broadcast of a libel where it had no effective control over the maker of the statement.

An internet service provider, or other provider or operator of a communications system, will not have primary responsibility for a statement transmitted by a person over which it has no effective control.

The situations can be extended by analogy.

The crux is essentially whether the defendant has responsibility for content or the decision to publish.

Reasonable care and reason to believe

In determining whether a person without primary responsibility took reasonable care in relation to a publication, regard should be had to the following:

(a) the extent of that person's responsibility for the content of the statement or the decision to publish;

(b) the nature or circumstances of the publication;

(c) The previous conduct or character of the author, editor or publisher (if the publication in question is notorious for its involvement in libel actions the defendant will be expected to be more vigilant in checking for defamatory material than in the case of more innocuous publications).

If a party is put on notice that it is involved in the publication of defamatory material, it may not be able to rely on this defence for acts of publication which took place after notice was given. The notification must be sufficiently convincing to make a reasonable person have reason to believe that the material is defamatory. This will be a question of fact in each case.

Offer of amends

Sections 2–4 of the Defamation Act 1996 introduces a new procedure whereby a defendant can offer to make a public correction of a defamatory statement, to make an apology and to pay compensatory damages in order to compromise litigation at an early stage before service of the defence. The exact procedure for making an offer of amends is beyond the remit of this book. If an offer of amends is made, and rejected by the defendant, the fact that the offer was made will be a complete defence to the proceedings unless the plaintiff can show that the defendant knew or ought to have known that the statement in question was false and defamatory of the plaintiff and that the statement would have been likely to have been understood to refer to him.

Who can sue for defamation?

Individuals and companies can sue. The amount of damages awarded to companies is generally lower than for individuals. Companies cannot recover damages for distress and hurt feelings, whereas individuals can. These elements can make up a substantial part of an individual plaintiff's damages.

Political parties cannot sue, nor can local authorities, government bodies or nationalised industries – although individual officials can sue if a statement would be understood to refer to them personally. Dead people cannot sue for defamation.

TRADE LIBEL AND MALICIOUS FALSEHOOD

Unlike the law of defamation, which protects reputation, the law of trade libel provides a remedy for untrue and malicious statements which disparage a competitor's goods or services but which do not necessarily reflect upon reputation. Trade libel is a species of the cause of action known as *malicious* (sometimes also called *injurious*) *falsehood*.

The distinction between defamation and trade libel

Disparagement of a business's goods does not always damage its reputation, for example, to write that Y's goods do not taste good is unlikely to damage Y's reputation and will not therefore be defamatory. It may, however, be a malicious falsehood or a trade libel.

The elements of trade libel/malicious falsehood

The plaintiff must prove the following:
(a) the words complained of refer to the plaintiff;
(b) the words about which complaint is made are false;
(c) they were published maliciously; and
(d) as a direct result of the publication of the statement the defendant has suffered financial loss.

The loss that is compensated by this cause of action is financial loss. Compensation for hurt and distress or loss of reputation is not recoverable.

False statement

Often the consideration of whether a statement is false involves consideration of the meaning of the statement, taking into account the inferences and any innuendo meaning of the statement. The same difficulties can arise as in relation to defamation (see above).

The meaning of malice

Malice has the same meaning as in relation to defamation actions (see above, p 48). Generally, it involves showing that the words in question were published in the knowledge that they were untrue or without care as to whether they were true or not.

Some special considerations in relation to comparative advertising

There have been a number of important cases involving claims of malicious falsehood in the field of comparative advertising. The cases have involved allegations that the comparative advertisements in question contain untrue statements about a competitor's goods and services.

When construing the claims made in comparative advertisements, the court will be concerned to determine what the reasonable man would find the claim to mean and whether a reasonable man would take the claims made in the advertising to be made seriously. If they would be taken with a pinch of salt no cause of action would arise.

A detailed examination of the approach which has been taken by the courts in interpreting comparative advertisements can be found in Chapters 1 and 8. They should be read in conjunction with the points set out below.

(a) The court will not always make a minute, word for word analysis of the content of an advertisement. In recognition of the way that the majority of people would consider an advertisement, the court will take a more broad brush approach – see the commentary on the *Barclays v RBS Advanta* judgment in Chapter 1 for more detail.

(b) The court will make an allowance for puffery (exaggerated claims which are not intended to be taken seriously). It will ask: would the reasonable man take the claim seriously? If so, the claim may be a trade libel if it is unsupported by evidence.

(c) The use of puffery will not in itself make an advertisement dishonest or the claims made false – see the discussion of *Vodafone Group plc v Orange Personal Communications Limited* in Chapter 1.

(d) The advertisement should be considered as a whole, for example, constituent parts of a mailshot should be read together – *Barclays v RBS Advanta*.

Each advertisement should be considered on its own merits. What would be understood as mere puffery by a reasonable man in an advertisement for, say, soap powder might be taken seriously in an advertisement for a pharmaceutical product. This was illustrated in the case of *Ciba-Geigy plc v Parke Davis and Co Limited* [1994] FSR 8.

The case concerned comparative advertising of competing drugs. The judge observed:

> I have no doubt that statements such as A's flour is as good as B's or A's flour can be substituted in all recipes for B's flour are puffs and are not actionable. However that does not mean that a similar statement would be a puff and not actionable if made in relation to a pharmaceutical product. Parliament has thought it necessary to regulate the sale of pharmaceutical products in ways which have not been applied to flour and therefore the common law could apply different standards to statements about pharmaceuticals to those made about flour.

The more specific or precise a statement is, the more likely that it will be taken to mean what it literally says, as opposed to be conveying a more general message.

The case of *De Beers Abrasive Products Limited v International General Electric Co of New York Limited* [1975] 2 All ER 599 concerned a pamphlet which was presented to be a scientific comparison of the plaintiff's and the defendant's products. The case laid down the principle that the proper test to determine whether a statement is puffery or whether it has overstepped the line between puffery and denigration is whether the reasonable man would take the claim being made seriously. It was held that, because the defendant's pamphlet gave the impression that it was a scientific test, it would not be regarded as puffery.

Avoiding liability for trade libel/malicious falsehood

(a) Do not denigrate a competitor or its products/services unless the claims can be supported by evidence of a kind that will be admissible in court. In the *Vodafone* case, the claims made in the advertising that on average Orange users save £20 per month compared to Vodafone's equivalent tariff was made after extensive research had been carried out to support that assertion.

(b) Have the proof to support your claim in place before the claim is published, to avoid any suggestion of malice.

(c) Exaggerated statements such as 'Best Value on the Market' will not give rise to a cause of action provided that the reasonable audience would not, in the opinion of the court, take the statement seriously. Ensure that such statements will be clearly interpreted as puffery rather than as assertions of fact.

(d) Avoid specific statements, for example, 'X washing powder lasts longer than Y washing powder', unless there is evidence to support them. Instead, opt for a formula such as 'Best Value Powder', which is more likely to be interpreted as puffery. However, bear in mind that under the industry codes, for example, the CAP codes, statements which amount to puffery are likely to be found to contravene the codes where there is no evidence to support them. Even though there may be no liability for trade libel, the advertisement may still be a breach of the codes.

(e) The nature of the product that is being advertised may affect how seriously advertising claims are taken. Care should be taken when advertising pharmaceutical products or when making claims based on scientific results.

(f) Even if a trade competitor is not named, advertisements may still give rise to a cause of action if the reasonable audience would understand it to refer to the competitor.

The internet

The principles of the law of defamation and malicious falsehood apply to the internet as they do to other media. It is possible to publish material on the internet which is read worldwide. This has two main implications.

The first is the potential for material which is published on the internet to reach a vast worldwide readership. As a general rule, the greater the extent of publication, the greater will be the exposure to a large award of damages.

The second implication is the exposure to libel proceedings in different territories across the world. Depending on the national laws of each State where publication takes place, that is, where downloading of the material occurs, it may be possible for the person who alleges that they have been defamed to launch proceedings in each of those territories.

Criminal libel

The making of defamatory statements can be an offence under criminal law where the statements are sufficiently serious to warrant the institution of criminal proceedings. Prosecutions for criminal libel are extremely rare and are only brought where the public interest requires it, for example, where the statement is likely to provoke a breach of the peace or to pervert the course of justice. Neither of these scenarios is likely to occur in an advertising or sales promotion context!

The publication of a defamatory libel is punishable by imprisonment of up to 12 months and/or a fine. Publication in the knowledge that the statement is false is punishable by imprisonment of up to two years and/or a fine.

Limitation periods

Actions for defamation and malicious falsehood/trade libel must generally be brought within 12 months from the date of publication of the statement. Each separate publication must be taken into account, for example, in the case of a TV commercial, each broadcast will constitute a fresh publication from which the 12 month period will run. In Scotland, unlike the rest of the UK, the limitation period is three years from the date of publication.

Insurance

Actions for defamation and trade libel tend to be very expensive to defend. Because of the nature of the causes of action it is difficult to clear material with certainty. Advertisers who are worried about their potential exposure to claims should consider taking out insurance to safeguard themselves against large awards of damages and costs.

CHAPTER 4

COPYRIGHT

The law of copyright is contained in an Act of Parliament, the Copyright, Designs and Patents Act 1988 (the Act).

What is copyright?

Copyright is a property right. It exists in original products (known as works) and enables the copyright owner to restrain certain unauthorised acts in relation to those works. Copyright exists independently of the work itself. The owner of the work will not necessarily own the copyright, and vice versa.

The acts which the copyright owner can prevent others from doing are as follows:

(a) Copying the work.

(b) Issuing copies of the work to the public.

(c) Performing, playing or showing the work in public.

(d) Broadcasting the work or including it in a cable programme service.

(e) Making an adaptation of the work or doing any of the above acts in relation to an adaptation.

If the above activities are carried out without the copyright owner's permission, copyright in the work will be infringed.

In the UK, the copyright owner is not required to register its copyright. Copyright arises automatically.

More information about copyright works

Copyright will exist in *original* works of the following types:

(a) *Literary works*; any work other than a dramatic or musical work (see below) which is spoken, written or sung. Literary works can include text, computer programs, mathematical tables, compilations, advertising copy, scripts, screenplays, and lyrics to songs or jingles. Coupons for competitions and cards containing a sequence of varying grids and lines for use in a competition have been held to be literary works.

(b) *Dramatic works*; including stage plays, dances and mime.

(c) *Musical works*; music of all kinds; including arrangements of existing music and jingles. The lyrics to a song will be a literary work. The tune itself will be a musical work.

(d) *Artistic works*; photographs, illustrations, paintings, drawings, storyboards (although the language elements will be classed as literary works), sculptures, models, signatures.

(e) *Sound recordings*; sounds embodied in recordings. The sounds may be literary works or musical works in their own right.

(f) *Films*; feature films, newsreels, home videos, animatics, television programmes, filmed advertisements.

(g) *Broadcasts*; including analogue, digital, terrestrial and satellite broadcasts. All are protected independently of the programmes or advertisements contained in the broadcast.

(h) *Cable programmes*; items transmitted on cable programme services. As with broadcasts, the subject of the broadcast will have its own copyright.

(i) *Databases*; a collection of independent works or data arranged in a systematic or methodical way and individually accessible by electronic or other means.

An important concept to grasp is that there can be more than one copyright in a work. An advertisement may consist of illustrations and copy. The illustrations will be artistic works in their own right and the copy will be a literary work. A film is a copyright work in its own right but it is also made up of separate copyright works such as the script (literary work), the sound track (sound recording) and the music (musical work). If it is broadcast on television, the broadcast will have a separate copyright to the film and its constituent elements. Copyright in each of these types of work may be owned by a separate entity.

Originality

In order to qualify for copyright protection, a work has to be original. This does not mean that it has to be unique. Originality simply means that the work must have been independently created or, to put it the other way round, that it has not been copied from something else. The creation of the work must also have involved the creator in the exercise of some degree of skill, judgment and labour.

Databases are original if the database constitutes the author's own intellectual creation by reason of the selection or arrangement of the database contents.

Copyright is not a monopoly

Copyright protects to restrain the *copying* of the work in which it subsists. It does not grant a monopoly in the work. A party can independently create an identical work and, if the design was not copied, copyright will not have been infringed.

Fixation

Copyright will not subsist in a literary, dramatic or musical work unless the work is recorded in a material form, for example, in writing or stored in a computer.

Example

Where a speech is made *ad lib*, that is, without written notes or text, copyright will not exist in the speech as a literary work unless and until it is recorded, for example, by the taking of written notes of the speech or by the making of a sound recording.

Copyright in ideas

It is often said that copyright does not exist in ideas, but only in the form in which ideas are expressed. Often this proves to be true. However, the maxim is too glib to be accepted at face value and requires qualification. A more accurate reflection of the law is that copyright will exist where the work is in a sufficiently concrete form to attract protection. If the work is too nebulous or imprecise, it will not enjoy copyright protection. A general idea or a basic concept is unlikely to be protected by copyright. However, ideas which develop the general or basic concept can be protected by copyright provided that they are recorded in material form. Anyone can use the basic idea or underlying concept but, if they copy the detail, they may infringe copyright. The distinction between the basic and the detailed is often a difficult one to draw.

Example

In the case of *Green v Broadcasting Corporation of New Zealand* [1989] 2 All ER 1056, Hughie Green, the compere of the well known talent show called Opportunity Knocks, commenced proceedings for copyright infringement against New Zealand Broadcasting Corporation over the broadcast of a similar show.

Mr Green claimed that he was the owner of copyright in the scripts and dramatic format of Opportunity Knocks. However, detailed scripts were not produced in evidence, nor was a written format produced. Instead, the court heard evidence that the scripts/format consisted of a number of catch phrases used in each show, the use of a device known as a clapometer and other general ideas.

The court found that in the absence of detailed scripts the plaintiff was doing no more than seeking to protect the general idea or concept for his talent show and that such a nebulous concept could not be protected by copyright.

The protection of rights in formats is considered in more detail in Chapter 11.

Copyright in titles and slogans

A literary work for which copyright protection is sought may be original and its creation may have involved the expenditure of skill, judgment and labour, but still it might not enjoy copyright protection if it does not have certain qualities. Those qualities were characterised in the case of *Exxon Corp v Exxon Insurance Consultants* [1982] Ch 119 as the conveying of information, the provision of instruction or the giving of pleasure.

In the *Exxon* case, it was held that copyright did not subsist in the word Exxon (which was part of the plaintiff's corporate name) on the basis that the word was simply an artificial combination of four letters of the alphabet which served a purpose only when used in juxtaposition with other English words to identify one or other companies in the plaintiff group. It did not have any of the necessary qualities which were required for copyright to subsist.

Copyright in titles and slogans

Copyright is highly unlikely to subsist in titles and slogans on the basis that they are too insubstantial to be deserving of such protection or that they do not satisfy the criteria laid down in the *Exxon* case.

Copyright in conversations

A conversation is theoretically capable of copyright protection as a literary work provided that it is recorded. Copyright in the conversation will belong to the speakers either jointly (as joint authors of the conversation) or separately in relation to each individual's words. The conversation must have involved the expenditure of skill, judgment and labour. It must meet the criteria set out in the *Exxon* case by conveying information, providing instruction or giving pleasure. A commonplace conversation is unlikely to satisfy these criteria, although the author is not aware of a decided case on the point. Attempts have been made to rely on copyright in answers given during interviews to prevent the unauthorised use of television interview footage, although no such case has yet proceeded to trial.

Duration of copyright – a guide

Copyright does not subsist in a work indefinitely. The provisions relating to the duration of copyright are technical and not without difficulty. The position can be summarised as follows:

(a) Copyright in *literary works, artistic works, dramatic works* and *musical works* will expire *70 years* after the end of the calendar year in which the author dies.

(b) In the case of *films,* copyright expires *70 years* from the end of the calendar year after the death of the last of the following persons (or the last of the following persons whose identity is known):

- the principal director;
- the writer of the screenplay;
- the dialogue writer;
- the writer of music commissioned for the film and used in the film.

(c) Copyright in *sound recordings* expires *50 years* from the end of the calendar year in which the recording was first released or 50 years from the making of the recording if it is not released within 50 years.

(d) Copyright in *broadcasts and cable* expires *50 years* from the year of first inclusion in a cable programme.

(e) In the case of *computer generated works* copyright expires *50 years* from the end of the calendar year when the work was first made.

(f) Where *artistic works* are *exploited industrially* the term of copyright protection will be reduced to 25 years.

The above is a guide only to what are complex provisions. For further detail, the reader is referred to ss 12–15A of the Act as amended by the Duration of Copyright and Rights in Performances Regulations 1995.

Who owns copyright?

The basic rule is that the first owner of copyright will be the creator (or *author*) of the work.

Joint ownership

Where there is more than one author, copyright will be owned jointly.

In order to qualify as a joint author, a person has to play an active part in the creation of the work. Merely criticising or commenting on the author's early drafts will not in itself confer rights in the work.

Copyright in literary, dramatic, musical or artistic works (other than computer generated works) which are created by joint authors will expire 70 years after the death of the last of the joint authors whose identity is known.

Commissioned works

Where a work is commissioned then, in the absence of any agreement to the contrary, copyright vests in the creator of the work, *not the commissioner.*

Example

If a client commissions and pays an advertising agency to devise a poster, copyright in the artistic and literary works which may make up the poster will belong to the agency. The fact that the agency is paid in full for its work will not affect this position. The client may own the physical property, that is, the original artwork for the poster, but the copyright will belong to the agency.

If the agency commissions a photographer to take pictures for the poster, copyright in the photographs will belong to the photographer, irrespective of who owns the physical property.

The commissioner is not therefore the automatic owner of copyright in material which it commissions. If copyright is to be acquired in the material, it will have to be transferred by way of assignment.

Often the identity of the author will be obvious. In relation to certain categories of work, the Act identifies 'author' to mean the following:

(a) *Computer generated works* – the author is the person who undertakes the arrangements for their creation.

(b) *Sound recordings* – the author is the person who undertakes the arrangements for the recording – generally the producer or record company.

(c) *Films* – the author is the person who undertakes the arrangements for the filming – generally this will be the film producer. The law provides that copyright is co-owned by the producer and the principal director.

(d) *Broadcasts* – copyright is owned jointly by the entity making the broadcast where that entity has responsibility for content *and* the programme provider which contracts for its transmission.

(e) *Cable broadcasts* – copyright is owned by the programme provider.

Unknown authors

The identity of the author is to be regarded as unknown if it is not possible to identify the author by reasonable inquiry.

Where the author is unknown, copyright will expire in a literary, dramatic, musical or artistic work (other than a computer generated work) 70 years from the end of the calendar year in which the work was made or if the work has been made available to the public within the 70 year period at the end of 70 years from the end of the calendar year when the work was first made available.

The position of employees

Where employees, as part of their duties, create works, copyright will belong to the employer unless there is provision to the contrary.

If the work is created outside of the employee's normal duties, even if during office hours, copyright will belong to the employee unless it has been agreed otherwise.

Where freelance staff create copyright works, they will own copyright. Copyright assignments will be required from such staff. Whenever there is a doubt about whether someone is an employee or freelance, assignments should be taken.

Subsequent owners of copyright

The author will be the first owner of copyright. Often copyright is acquired by third parties. It should not be assumed that the author of a copyright work has retained his/her copyright. The lack of a central copyright register can make it difficult to identify the owners of copyright. This often makes it difficult to obtain permission to use the copyright work. In some cases, clearance is made easier by the existence of collecting societies.

Collecting societies

Many copyright owners allow collecting societies to administer their copyright on their behalf for reasons of convenience. Collecting societies administer hundreds of similar copyrights for different authors. In some cases, the copyright owner is required as a condition of membership to assign its copyright to the agency which will then exercise it on behalf of the author for example, by taking legal proceedings in respect of infringement, by granting consents and by collecting royalties on behalf of the author. Often, it is the relevant collecting society which is authorised to grant a licence for the use of, for example, a piece of music, rather than the author of the work.

The principal collecting societies are as follows:

(a) *Performing rights* are administered by the Performing Rights Society (PRS). Performing rights are the rights to perform literary, dramatic, artistic and musical works in public.

(b) *Phonographic rights* are administered by Phonographic Performance Limited (PPL). Phonographic rights are the rights to broadcast or perform sound recordings in public.

(c) *Video performance rights* are administered by Video Performance Limited (VPL). Video performance rights are the rights to broadcast or perform music videos in public.

(d) *Synchronisation rights* are administered by the Mechanical Copyright Protection Society (MCPS). Synchronisation rights are the rights to record music and to synchronise it with a film.

Transferring copyright

Like other types of property, copyright can be transferred. Such a transaction is known as an *assignment.* Assignments must be in writing and signed by the assignor (the person transferring the copyright) in order to be fully effective. The assignment should be for consideration (usually a payment, however nominal).

Assignments can transfer copyright in works which are not in existence at the time of assignment. Such an assignment is known as a present assignment of future copyright.

Assignments can also be limited in the sense that they can transfer copyright for a limited period or in respect of certain territories only or for specified purposes.

Licences

A licence is permission by the copyright owner (*the licensor*) to a third party (*the licensee*) permitting the licensee to make use of its copyright material in circumstances which would otherwise be an infringement of copyright. A licence does not transfer ownership of copyright.

Licences can be exclusive or non-exclusive.

An exclusive licence is in some ways similar to an assignment in that, whilst not transferring ownership of copyright, it gives the licensee the sole and exclusive right to do the acts which are the subject of the licence to the exclusion of anyone else. An exclusive licensee is able to bring proceedings to restrain copyright infringement, although it will generally have to join the copyright owner as a party to the proceedings.

A non-exclusive licensee will not have exclusive rights to use of the copyright granted in the licence, nor will it be able to sue in its own name for copyright infringement.

An exclusive licence must be in writing and signed by the licensor. A non-exclusive licence can be oral but, as with any agreement, it is advisable to have the terms set down in writing and signed by both parties, in order to be certain about what has been agreed by the parties.

Ownership of copyright in advertising material

Advertisers will have seen that they will not automatically acquire copyright in advertising material which they commission from third parties. If they wish to acquire copyright in such material, they will have to take an assignment of copyright from the copyright owner.

Where the agency has itself subcontracted the work, for example, to a film production company or a composer, an assignment will be required from those parties. In relation to some types of material, it is not standard practice to assign copyright, for example, specially commissioned photographs or music (such as jingles). In such cases, assignments of copyright are likely to involve payment of a large sum of money by the advertiser to the copyright owner.

It is usual for an agreement between client and advertising agency to contain a provision that the agency will assign such copyright that it owns in material that it produces on the client's behalf. Such a clause will not oblige the agency to obtain copyright from third parties which it commissions to do work on behalf of the client.

Where the advertiser wishes to acquire copyright in all material including work which the agency subcontracts to third parties, the contract between the agency and client should expressly oblige the agency to undertake to acquire copyright from third parties.

If an assignment of copyright material is not taken, the advertiser must take a licence from the copyright owner for use of the copyright work. Failure to do so may result in proceedings for copyright infringement. The fact that a photographer is commissioned to take photographs may not in itself constitute a licence to use the pictures. A licence to use the material should be obtained as part of the agreement with the photographer or by way of a separate agreement.

Material created for pitches

Ownership of copyright can be of particular relevance in relation to materials created for advertising pitches or beauty parades. The case of *Hutchison*

Personal Communications Limited v Hook Advertising Limited [1995] FSR 365 offers a warning of the difficulties that can arise if ownership of copyright in materials created for the pitch is not determined at the time of the pitch.

Hook Advertising Limited created a logo for Hutchison as part of a pitch for Hutchison's business. Hook's pitch was successful and a contract between the parties was drawn up which provided that copyright in all material produced or created by Hook for Hutchison's advertising would belong to Hutchison.

A dispute subsequently arose between the agency and the client about ownership of the logo. Hook argued that Hutchison did not own copyright in the logo under the contract terms referred to above because it had been created before Hook's appointment as Hutchison's agents. The court found that the words 'produced and created' for Hutchison's advertising did *not* cover material produced for the pitch. The words only covered material which originated during the term of Hook's appointment.

Special provision should therefore be made for material which originates outside an agent's term of appointment.

Infringement and how to avoid it

A person who, without the licence of the copyright owner, does or authorises another to do any of the following acts (known as the restricted acts), infringes copyright:

(a) copies the work;

(b) issues copies of the work to the public;

(c) performs, plays or shows the work in public;

(d) broadcasts the work or includes the work in a cable television service;

(e) makes an adaptation of a work or does any of the above in relation to an adaptation.

These acts of infringement are known as primary *infringements*. It is no defence to an allegation of primary infringement that the infringement was accidental (although it may serve to reduce the amount of damages payable).

We shall consider the acts of primary infringement in turn.

Copying the work

Copying includes reproduction of the work in any material form, including storing the work in any medium by electronic means. In relation to an artistic work it includes the making of a three-dimensional copy of a two-dimensional work and vice versa.

Copying in relation to a film, television broadcast or cable programme includes making a photograph of the whole or a substantial part of any image forming part of the film or programme.

A copy can be an exact copy of the copyright work. It can also be a copy of a substantial part of the work. Substantiality is a qualitative test rather than a quantitative test, depending on the importance of what has been copied rather than the quantity. The part copied can be a relatively small part of the work, but if it is important to the work as a whole it may still infringe copyright. Sometimes people talk of a percentage cut off point, for example, 'we won't infringe copyright if we only copy 10% of the work'. Such an approach is wrong in law and *should never be relied on*, even as a rule of thumb. Instead, the overall importance of the part that is reproduced must be considered.

Similarity is an objective test. It involves asking whether the reasonable person would conclude that the defendant has reproduced a substantial part of the plaintiff's work. The subjective opinions of the parties are not conclusive. The degree of similarity required can relate to the overall effect of the works as well as to the individual features.

The issue of what is substantial is a question of degree.

Where the work concerns a commonplace subject which is presented in a straightforward manner, only an exact reproduction of it, or something that is almost an exact reproduction, will constitute an infringement.

Example

In the case of *Kenrick v Lawrence* (1890) 25 QBD 93, the plaintiff claimed copyright in the representation of a hand marking a cross on an electoral voting paper. There was nothing artistically significant in the representation. The court held that, where a drawing depicts a simple operation which must be performed by everyone who votes, there was not an exclusive right to represent that operation. Nothing more than a literal copy would suffice to establish copyright infringement.

Parodies

To what extent can a parody be an infringement of copyright?

Parodies by their nature will involve the exercise of skill, judgment and labour in their creation. They will, however, usually involve a reference to, or incorporation of, a copyright work. Is a parody a copyright work in its own right or an infringement of the earlier work?

The question was considered in the case of *Williamson Music v Pearson Partnership* [1987] FSR 97, where an advertising agency produced an advertisement for a bus company which parodied the lyrics and music of the Rogers and Hammerstein song *There Is Nothing Like A Dame*.

The plaintiffs brought proceedings for copyright infringement in the song.

The court found an arguable case that there was infringement in the music to the song (but not the lyrics).

It was held that the relevant test to apply was whether the author of the parody had reproduced a substantial part of the copyright work. The fact that the defendant may have used mental labour to produce something original, or some part of which was original, was irrelevant if the resulting parody reproduced without licence a substantial part of the copyright work.

How to establish that copying has taken place

Similarity or substantial similarity will not in itself be sufficient to give rise to copyright infringement unless copying can be established. If the defendant's product is the work of independent research or the similarity is due to coincidence, copyright will not be infringed.

The fact that copying must have taken place can be inferred from the surrounding circumstances (for example, if the defendant's work incorporates errors contained in the plaintiff's works which the defendant is highly unlikely to have made without having had sight of the plaintiff's work). Where the plaintiff and defendant's works are identical, or very similar, the onus of proof of establishing that the defendant's work is his/her independent creation will in practice be on the defendant (for example, by showing that he/she never had access to the plaintiff's work or that his/her work predates the plaintiff's work).

Copying can be subconscious. The copyist may not be aware of having seen, read or heard the plaintiff's work but he can still have copied it. To establish subconscious copying the onus is on the plaintiff to prove the notoriety of its work in order to show that the defendant must have been familiar with it.

Issuing copies of the work to the public

It is the first act of putting the copies into circulation which falls within this provision. The copies must therefore be copies which have not previously been put into circulation anywhere in the world. There is an exception to this general rule in relation to sound recordings: films or computer programmes in respect of which 'issuing to the public' includes renting copies of such works to the public.

Any subsequent distribution, including import of goods originating outside the UK into the jurisdiction, will be a *secondary infringement* of copyright (see below, p 70).

Performance of the work in public

The unauthorised performance in public of a literary, dramatic, or musical work, whether by means of sound recording, film, broadcast or cable programme, will infringe copyright in the work in question.

Similarly, the playing or showing in public of a sound recording, film, broadcast or cable programme will infringe copyright in such a work.

The making of an adaptation of the work

An adaptation includes the making of a translation of the work or an alteration in its form, for example, a translation of a novel which is converted into a play or a screenplay.

If an adaptation is made without consent it will infringe copyright in the work.

The adaptation itself, if made with the authority of the copyright owner, may have its own copyright, for example, a translation will be protected by copyright as a literary work in its own right provided that the translator has expended skill, judgment and labour on its creation.

An arrangement or transcription of a musical work will qualify as an adaptation and must therefore be authorised by the copyright owner.

It is an infringement of the adapted work to carry out any of the restricted acts in relation to the adaptation.

Authorisation of infringing acts

It is an infringement of copyright to authorise a third party to commit an infringing act. Authorisation means more than mere facilitation of the infringement. In order to authorise a copyright infringement, the authoriser must grant or purport to grant the *right* to carry out the act of infringement. The purported grant can only come from someone purporting to have the authority to make the grant.

In the case of *CBS Songs v Amstrad* [1988] RPC 567, it was alleged that Amstrad, who were manufacturers of a twin deck tape recorder, had authorised purchasers to infringe copyright in sound recordings by making available to the public the means for cassette tapes to be recorded onto blank cassette tapes. The court held that the mere enabling of the infringement brought about by the supply of the equipment did not amount to authorisation. There was no purported grant of the right to make the illicit recordings.

Secondary infringement

Unlike primary infringement, acts of secondary infringement will only infringe copyright where the infringer knows or has reason to believe that the work with which he is dealing is an infringing copy.

'Reason to believe' involves knowledge by the defendants of such facts as would lead the reasonable person to suspect that he/she is dealing with infringing copies.

Acts of secondary infringement

The acts set out below are secondary infringements if done without the consent of the copyright owner:

(a) importation into the UK of articles known by the defendant to be an infringing copy of the work or where the defendant has reason to believe that it is an infringement; or

(b) possession in the course of business;

(c) selling, hiring, offering or exposing for sale or hire;

(d) exhibition in public in the course of business;

(e) distribution in the course of business;

(f) distribution not in the course of business but to an extent as to affect prejudicially the owner of the copyright,

of any article which the defendant knows or has reason to believe is an infringing copy.

Making, importing into the UK, possessing in the course of a business, or selling or hiring or offering to do so, an article specifically designed or adapted for making copies is also a secondary infringement where there is knowledge or reason to believe that the apparatus will be used to make infringing copies.

Secondary infringements in relation to public performance

In relation to primary infringements by the performance of a literary, dramatic or musical work in public (see above, p 69), the person who gave permission for a place of public entertainment to be used for the performance will be liable for secondary infringement unless when he gave permission he believed on reasonable grounds that the performance would not infringe copyright.

Where the performance or the playing or showing of the work in public is carried out by means of relevant equipment, such as equipment for playing sound recordings, the person supplying the apparatus will be liable where he knew or had reason to believe that the apparatus was likely to be used to infringe copyright. The same is true for occupiers of premises who gave permission for the apparatus to be brought onto the premises. Where the apparatus is of the kind normally used for public performances, the person supplying the apparatus must show that he did not believe on reasonable grounds that it would be used to infringe copyright.

A person who supplies a copy of a sound recording or a film used to infringe copyright, for example, by an unauthorised showing in public, will be liable for infringement if, when he supplied it, he knew or had reason to believe that it (or a copy made from it) was likely to be used to infringe copyright.

Permitted uses of copyright works

In some circumstances, the restricted acts can be carried out in relation to copyright works without infringing copyright. There are numerous circumstances set out in the Act. This book sets out only the most relevant to advertisers and promoters. There must have been a 'fair dealing' in relation to the permitted acts.

The fair dealing provisions

Where the use of a copyright work amounts to a 'fair dealing' for certain specified purposes known as 'permitted acts', it will not infringe copyright. The circumstances that can amount to fair dealing are set out in the Act.

What is a fair dealing?

The concept of fair dealing is flexible. Whether a particular use is a fair dealing will depend on such factors as the amount of the copyright work that has been taken, including the number and extent of any quotations, and the proportion that the copyright work bears to independent material. Are there too many extracts from the copyright work and are the extracts too long to be 'fair'? If the copyright work is unpublished, or has a restricted circulation, it may make it harder to rely on the fair dealing defence.

What are the permitted acts?

The permitted acts are set out in the Act as follows:

(a) Fair dealing with a literary, dramatic, musical or artistic work for the purposes of research or private study.

(b) Fair dealing with a work for the purpose of criticism or review of that work or of another work or of a performance of the work, provided that it is accompanied by a sufficient acknowledgment (defined below).

(c) Fair dealing with a work *other than a photograph* for the purpose of reporting current events, provided that it is accompanied by a sufficient acknowledgment (this is not necessary in connection with reporting current events by means of a sound recording, film broadcast or cable programme). The phrase 'current events' does not extend to current affairs. It applies to specific and recent happenings. It does not apply to general discussion on matters that are currently of public interest.

What is a sufficient acknowledgment?

A sufficient acknowledgment is a notice which must identify the work in question by its title or other description and also identify the author of the work (unless it is published anonymously or it is not possible to ascertain the identity of the author by reasonable inquiry). It is unnecessary to include an expression of thanks in the acknowledgment. The acknowledgment should be sufficiently prominent that it will be recognised by reasonably alert members of the relevant audience.

Incidental inclusion

If a copyright work is included in a film, sound recording or artistic work in an incidental way, permission from the copyright owner is not required for the inclusion. The term 'incidental' is undefined. The author suggests that the protection is unlikely to extend to the deliberate inclusion of a copyright work, even if its impact is peripheral to the main action. Certainly, the Act provides that a musical work will not be regarded as incidentally included where it has been deliberately included, for example, as background music.

Contemporaneous notes of a speaker

If a record is made of the words uttered by a speaker, the speaker may have copyright in his words. This situation could have adverse effects on the reporting of current events on television and radio. The speaker could theoretically use his copyright to restrain the broadcast of his words. In order to prevent such a situation arising, the Act provides that where the speaker's words have been recorded directly, the person with lawful possession of the record can use it for the reporting of current events or in a broadcast or cable programme without infringing the speaker's copyright in his words, provided that the making of the record was not prohibited by the speaker before it was made.

Public interest

Where copyright infringement is justifiable in the public interest, that fact will be a defence to any claim of infringement. This defence overrides the rights of the copyright owner. It is rarely successful, being limited to infringements involving material which is of importance to the public interest. It is, accordingly, unlikely to be of assistance in an advertising or promotions context.

Ways to protect copyright

(a) Mark copyright works with the © symbol. The symbol is not necessary to invoke copyright protection under UK law. It will, however, alert third parties to the fact that copyright is claimed in the work. The following formula should be used:

© Name of copyright owner and year of creation of the copyright work.

(b) Ensure that you *do* own copyright. Often businesses which commission material assume that they own copyright in it. As we have seen, that is not the case. Remember that copyright in material created by freelancers will belong to them unless copyright is assigned.

(c) Ensure that you can prove that your work is original. Keep all material which will demonstrate how the work was developed, including drafts, briefings, samples, any material on which the original concept was based, etc. Make a record of who worked on the project.

(d) Keep a record of the dates when the work was developed. You may have to prove that your work predates the work of alleged infringers.

How to avoid copyright infringement

Take a transfer of copyright in the material which you wish to use by way of assignment or obtain a licence to use the material. In either case, ensure that the assignor or licensor actually owns the copyright in question and that the assignment or licence is wide enough to cover all the uses to which the material will be put, the territories where it will be used and that it is of sufficient duration.

Remember that permission will not be needed where the fair dealing provisions apply.

Keep records

It is a good idea to keep records for all original works created, for example, earlier drafts, etc, to rebut any presumption of copying and to support the fact that the work is original.

What consents will be required – some special cases

The use of music

A piece of music or a song may contain a number of copyrights. A song may consist of lyrics and music. The lyrics will be a literary work and the tune will be a musical work. Different people might own the two copyrights. The song itself may be embodied in a sound recording. The sound recording will be a separate copyright work for which clearance will be required.

The rights to be cleared will typically consist of the following:

(a) Music/lyrics:

- The right to copy the works (known as the synchronisation right). This may be administered by MCPS or sometimes by PRS.
- The right to perform the work in public (which includes the right to broadcast the work). This right might be administered by PRS.

(b) Sound recordings:

- The right to copy the recording onto the soundtrack (known as dubbing the recording). In the first instance, the record company or producer should be approached and asked whether the dubbing right has been assigned.
- The right to perform the recording in public. This right might be administered by PPL.

In addition to the above, performers rights may need to be cleared. These are discussed below, p 76. Clearance can usually be carried out through the Musicians' Union. Any moral rights (see below, p 75) that have not been waived will also need to be considered.

The use of old footage

As with music, there are a number of copyright works which may be embodied in a film or television programme. In theory, clearance will be required in relation to each work. In addition to copyright in the footage itself, there may be copyright in the script and the set design to consider. If music is contained in the footage the rights in the music may have to be cleared separately (see above). Sometimes the above rights may have been assigned to the film/TV producer, which will simplify matters. Performers' rights will also need to be cleared. This can sometimes be achieved through Equity (the actors' union). Any moral rights that have not been waived will need to be considered.

Criminal offences

The Act sets out a number of criminal offences of copyright infringement.

It is a criminal offence to make for sale or hire, to import into the UK (other than for private use), to possess with a view to committing an infringing act, to sell, hire or offer or expose for sale or hire, to exhibit or to distribute an article which is *and which the defendant knows or has reason to believe is,* an infringement of copyright.

It is also an offence to make or possess an article designed to copy a particular copyright work knowing or having reason to believe that it will be used in relation to infringing works.

There are also related offences involving public performance of literary, dramatic and musical works and films.

The offences are punishable by fines or imprisonment.

Moral rights

Moral rights are separate to copyright. They belong to the author of a copyright work. They are personal rights which *cannot* be transferred. Upon the death of the owner they pass to his/her estate.

They are as follows:

(a) *The right of paternity*: this is the right to be credited as author or director of a work. The owner must assert this right in writing. The right does not apply to employees where the copyright in the work originally belongs to their employer.

(b) *The right of integrity*: this is the right to object to derogatory treatment in relation to the work. 'Treatment' means any adaptation of the work. 'Derogatory' is defined as any treatment which amounts to distortion or mutilation of the work or is otherwise prejudicial to the honour or reputation of the owner of the right. This right does *not* have to be asserted in writing to be effective.

(c) *The right against false attribution*. This right entitles the right owner not to have works falsely attributed to him/her.

(d) *The right of privacy in photographs/films taken for private or domestic purposes*. This right is considered in detail in Chapter 10.

Duration

Moral rights last for the duration of the copyright in the work in question, except in relation to the right against false attribution, which lasts until 20 years after the death of the owner.

Waiver

Moral rights cannot be assigned. They can be waived.

If an advertiser wishes to have unrestricted use of its advertising material, it should take steps to take the material free of moral rights. An assignment of copyright or a licence will not automatically waive moral rights. A waiver should be in writing, and signed by the owner of the right, to be effective. It is usual to express the waiver as being 'unconditional and irrevocable'.

Performers' rights

Whilst performers (for example, actors, voice-over artists, musicians) do not own copyright in their performances they will own property rights in the performances as follows:

(a) rental rights;

(b) reproduction rights;

(c) distribution rights.

The rights can be licensed or assigned in the same way as copyright.

The rights enable a performer to restrain the following unauthorised activities:

(a) The *rental and lending right* gives performers of works included in a film the right to authorise or prohibit the rental and lending of works containing their performances or including their works. They also receive an unalienable (that is, unassignable) right to equitable remuneration from the exploitation of their works.

    Equitable remuneration. Where the rental right has been assigned, the right to equitable remuneration will still apply. It cannot be transferred or waived. It is permissible to agree a one-off payment at the outset of a contract in respect of equitable remuneration, although any such payment will not necessarily prevent the performer asking for a larger sum in the future if the original payment does not turn out to have been 'equitable'.

(b) The *reproduction right* is the right of a performer to prevent any person making a copy of a recording of a substantial part of his performance without consent.

(c) The *distribution right* is the right of the performer to prevent any person issuing to the public copies of a substantial part of his performance without consent.

The performer also has rights to prevent unauthorised recordings of live performances, the right to authorise the use of a recording made without consent and the right to object to the importation, possession or to dealings with illicit recordings of his performance.

Wherever performers are used in advertising or promotional material, their written consent should be obtained to the use of their performance. This consent should extend to the voice of artists in voice-overs. The consent should be expressed to be irrevocable and in respect of all consents which are or may become necessary in the future.

CHAPTER 5

TRADE DESCRIPTIONS

The law which regulates the giving of false trade descriptions in advertisements and promotions is contained in the Trade Descriptions Act 1968 (the Act). The Act prohibits the misdescription of goods, services, accommodation and facilities. Non-compliance with the Act is a *criminal* offence. The law applying to the description of goods is different from the law applying to the description of services.

The Act applies to descriptions which are given in the course of trade or business.

Offences – goods

The Act creates three principal offences in relation to goods as follows:

(a) applying a false trade description to goods;

(b) supplying goods to which a false trade description has been applied;

(c) offering to supply goods to which a false trade description has been applied.

It is also an offence to do the following:

(a) to give a false indication that goods are of a kind supplied to third parties, such as celebrities;

(b) to make false representations that goods have royal approval.

What is a trade description?

A trade description is an indication of any of the following features of goods or parts of goods:

(a) quantity (which includes length, width, height, area, volume, capacity, weight and number), for example, a packet of sweets contains X number of chocolates;

(b) size;

(c) methods of manufacture, production, processing or reconditioning, for example, hand made;

(d) composition, including the way that goods are arranged – for example, representing goods as ready assembled when in fact they are supplied in kit form would be a false trade description;

(e) fitness for purpose, strength, performance, behaviour or accuracy, for example, representing goods as waterproof or suitable for cooking in a microwave oven;

(f) any other physical characteristics, for example, representing goods as environmentally friendly;

(g) any testing carried out in respect of the goods and its results;

(h) approval by any person or conformity with a type approved by any person, for example, the application of the Kite mark indicating conformity with the relevant British Standard;

(i) the person by whom the goods are manufactured, produced, processed or reconditioned and the place at or date of those activities;

(j) other history, including previous ownership or use.

The description can take the form of words, drawings, photographs, numbers, statements or any other indication of any of the features set out above.

What is a false trade description?

A false trade description is a description which is false *to a material degree*. Descriptions which are not strictly true are unlikely to be false to a material degree where the inaccuracy is trivial or minimal.

An example of a case where a description was not found to be false to a material degree is the case of *London Borough of Croydon v Premier Brands (UK) Limited* (Unreported, 8 and 9 February 1993) which concerned tea bags wrapped in a metallised plastic film. The product packaging stated that the tea bags were wrapped in *foil* for a fresher flavour. The description of 'foil' was challenged on the ground that metallised plastic was not 'foil'. The court held that the description was not false to a material degree. The public were themselves likely to refer to the packaging as foil whether the description was used or not.

Falsity extends to descriptions which, although not strictly untrue, are misleading. In the case of *Dixons Limited v Barnett* [1988] BTLC 311, the Dixons chain of stores sold a telescope which stated on its packaging that it offered 455 times magnification. The statement was strictly true. However, the 455 times magnification did not translate into useful vision. The maximum useful magnification was only 120 times. The court held that the description, whilst scientifically correct, was misleading to a material degree and therefore infringed the provisions of the Act.

There is no requirement for the prosecution to produce evidence of actual confusion in order to show that a description is false. However, the prosecution must prove that the statement *could* mislead.

Applying a trade description

The Act states that a person applies a trade description to goods if he:

(a) affixes or annexes it to or marks it on or incorporates the description with:

- the goods themselves; or
- anything in, on or with which the goods are supplied; or

(b) places the goods in, on or with anything which the trade description has been affixed or annexed to, marked on or incorporated with or places any such thing with the goods; or

(c) uses the trade description in any manner likely to be taken as referring to the goods.

These are very wide provisions which will include descriptions which are marked on:

(a) the goods themselves or their packaging;

(b) a label which is attached to the goods;

(c) descriptions made in advertisements;

(d) descriptions contained in promotional material such as product brochures;

(e) statements made orally as part of the sales process;

(f) descriptions contained in point of sale material.

Trade descriptions in advertisements can be false if the headlines and visuals give a false impression, even though the impression may be clarified elsewhere in the advertisement, for example, in the small print. Often the public does not take the trouble to read small print. There may be an exception to this general rule where the product in question is of a sophisticated or an expensive nature. The court may take the view that would-be purchasers would be likely to scrutinise sales material and advertisements in the case of such goods.

Example

In the case of *London Borough of Southwark v Time Computer Systems* (Unreported, 7 July 1997), a prosecution was brought in respect of an advertisement for a personal computer contained in a booklet which appeared in *What PC?* magazine. The advertisement gave the impression that the PC was preloaded with software and featured photographs of the boxes in which the software on offer as part of the package was normally supplied. A customer complained that when he received his PC, although he received the preloaded software, he did not receive the software boxes or the back-up disks and instruction manuals which would normally be inside the boxes. He was told that these items would be available at an extra cost. It was pointed out that the booklet stated at the foot of each page and in the endpiece that the boxes featured in the advertisements were for illustration only and that disks and manuals were available at extra cost.

A prosecution was brought alleging that the photographs of the boxes of software amounted to a false trade description that the software disks and manuals would be supplied with the PC. The prosecution failed. The court held that, in deciding whether a trade description was false to a material degree, it was entitled to take into account that the PC in question was a sophisticated and expensive piece of equipment. The advertisement was placed in a specialist magazine which was read predominantly by people who were intending to buy a computer. Such people would be likely to have regard to the small print in the advertisements. In the light of the nature of the advertisement in the brochure and the nature of the magazine in which it was contained, the pictorial representation did not amount to a false trade description.

Notwithstanding the above decision, it is recommended that advertisers take advice before putting important information in places where it is not immediately obvious. Even if the advertisement was not found to be a false trade description, it would, for example, be unlikely to find favour with the Advertising Standards Authority or other regulatory bodies.

Offering to supply goods to which a false trade description has been applied

This offence will be committed if goods to which a false description has been applied are sold or exposed for sale, for example, as part of a sales display. A person who has in his possession goods to which a false trade description has been applied, but who does not actually display them for sale, will commit an offence under this provision if the goods were in his possession for the purpose of being sold.

Trade descriptions in advertisements

Where a trade description is used in an advertisement in relation to a class of goods, it shall be taken as referring to all goods in that class whether they are in existence at the time that the advertisement is published or not. In determining whether any goods are of the class used in the advertisement, regard should be had to the form and content of the advertisement, the time, place, manner and frequency of its publication and all other matters making it likely or unlikely that a person to whom the goods are supplied would think of the goods as belonging to the class in question.

Who can be liable for the offences in relation to goods?

(a) *Application* – anyone in the chain of supply can be convicted of applying a false trade description, provided he applies the description in the course of business, for example, a manufacturer, wholesaler, retailer or importer.

(b) *Supply* – anyone who supplies goods in the course of business to which a false trade description has been applied can be guilty, whether or not he was responsible for the application of the description.

(c) *Offering to supply* – anyone offering to supply goods to which a false trade description has been applied can be guilty of offering to supply, whether or not he was responsible for the application of the original trade description.

Employees can be liable for acts committed in the course of their employment.

Penalties and enforcement

Where the case is dealt with summarily, a fine of up to £5,000 can be imposed for each offence. Where the case is heard on indictment, an unlimited fine and/or a term of imprisonment of up to two years may be given. Enforcement is by local Trading Standards Departments.

Strict liability

The offences in respect of goods are *strict liability* offences. This means that the intention of the person who commits the offence is irrelevant to the issue of liability (subject to the defences which are set out below). This position is to be contrasted with the offences relating to trade descriptions applied to services, accommodation and facilities. In those cases, the intention of the person making the trade description will be relevant.

The use of disclaimers

The inclusion of a disclaimer in a trade description can in some circumstances provide a defence to a charge of supplying or offering to supply goods to which a false trade description has been applied, but not to a charge of applying the false description. The disclaimer must be as prominent and compelling as the trade description itself and must be brought to the notice of the customer before he/she is committed to the purchase.

Defences

Innocent publication – a defence for commercial printers

It will be a defence to a person charged with an offence involving publication of an advertisement containing a false trade description to show that he is a person whose business it is to publish or arrange for the publication of advertisements and that he received the advertisement for publication in the ordinary course of business and did not know and had no reason to suspect that its publication would amount to an offence under the Act. 'Advertisement' includes a catalogue, circular, or price list.

Defence of mistake, accident etc

It is a defence for a person charged to show that the commission of the offence was due to:

(a) a mistake; or

(b) to reliance on information supplied to him; or

(c) to the act or default of another person, an accident or some other cause beyond his control,

provided that, in each case, he can also show that he took all reasonable precautions and exercised all due diligence to avoid the commission of the offence by himself or any person under his control.

The defence requires *all* reasonable steps to have been taken by the defendant and *all* due diligence to be exercised.

In practice, if the court is of the view that additional steps could reasonably have been taken to safeguard against breach, it is unlikely that the defence will be made out. The reader is referred to Chapter 6 concerning price indications for an analysis of the concept of 'due diligence'.

In relation to the offences of supplying and offering to supply goods to which a false trade description has been applied, it will be a defence for the person charged to prove that he did not know, and could not with reasonable diligence have ascertained, that the goods did not conform to the description or that the description had been applied to the goods.

Offences – services, accommodation and facilities

The offences considered above do not apply to services, accommodation and facilities. The following offence applies in their place.

It is an offence for any person in the course of trade or business to make a statement which he knows to be false or recklessly to make a statement that is false in relation to any of the following matters:

(a) the provision of any services, accommodation or facilities;

(b) the nature of any services, accommodation or facilities;

(c) the time at which, manner in which or persons by whom any services, accommodation or facilities are provided;

(d) the examination, approval or evaluation by any person of any services, accommodation or facilities;

(e) the location or amenities of any accommodation.

The meaning of reckless

A statement which is made regardless of whether it is true or false will be deemed to have been made recklessly.

The meaning of false

A statement is false if it is false to a material degree.

It is important in relation to descriptions relating to services, accommodation or facilities that there is a positive belief that they are true. Even if the descriptions are false, an offence under the Act will not have been committed if the description is genuinely believed to be correct. The law in relation to services is therefore not so strict as the law applying to the description of goods.

If it subsequently becomes known that a description was untrue at the time that it was made or that a description has become inaccurate, the maker of the statement will be obliged to correct the statement and to take steps to prevent anyone relying on it. In the case of *Wings Limited v Ellis* [1984] 1 All ER 1046, a holiday was advertised in a brochure as including air-conditioned accommodation. In fact, the accommodation was not air-conditioned. The holiday firm which advertised the holiday did not know that their description was false at the time that the advertisement was published. It subsequently came to their attention that there was no air-conditioning. They sent a memo to their staff alerting them to the mistake in the brochure. Despite this precaution a customer was not told of the lack of air-conditioning and complained that he had been misled. The court held that the company was guilty of making a false trade description which they knew to be false.

As in the case of goods, it is an offence to make false representations that services, accommodation or facilities have been supplied to a third party, for example, a celebrity, or that they are subject to royal approval.

CHAPTER 6

PRICE INDICATIONS

The principal law which regulates the giving of price indications in advertising and promotions is contained in Part III of the Consumer Protection Act 1987 (the Act). The Act is supported by a Code of Practice entitled the Code of Practice for Traders on Price Indications 1988, which is available free of charge from the Department of Trade and Industry.

The Act does not regulate the setting of price levels. Other areas of law might affect pricing policy, for example, competition law or the terms of a contract for the supply of goods. Such matters are beyond the scope of this book.

The Act prohibits the giving of misleading price indications. Under the Act, it is a *criminal* offence to give a price indication which is misleading.

What does the Act apply to?

The Act applies to price indications in respect of *all* goods and services.

What are the criminal offences which are created by the Act?

There are two offences created, as follows.

First offence – it is a criminal offence to give a misleading price indication to consumers about the price at which any goods or services are available either generally or from particular outlets.

Second offence – it is a criminal offence to give a price indication which, although correct at the time when it was first given, has subsequently become misleading and:

(a) some or all consumers might reasonably be expected to rely on the indication after it has become misleading; and

(b) the person responsible for the indication fails to take all such steps as are reasonable to prevent consumers from relying on it.

In order to avoid liability for the second offence, it is important to ensure that all price indications are up to date, for example, indications contained in sales literature or included in price lists should be monitored for accuracy. Where a price indication has become misleading, retailers should be prepared to cancel any transaction with a consumer who has relied on the price indication when making his or her decision to purchase.

Points to note about the offences

(a) Both offences can only be committed in the course of a business.

(b) Liability is limited to the owner of the business which gives the price indication. Employees cannot be liable under the Act for the giving of a misleading price indication.

(c) The price indication must be given to consumers. 'Consumer' is defined as a person who buys or might wish to buy goods or services for his or her private use or consumption. The Act does not extend to the purchase of goods and services for business purposes.

Penalties under the Act

An offender is liable to a fine up to a maximum of £5,000 on conviction in respect of each offence. Enforcement of the Act is the responsibility of local Trading Standards Departments.

The meaning of price

'Price' means the aggregate of the sums required to be paid by the consumer for goods or services or any method applied to calculate the aggregate figure.

The meaning of misleading

A price indication is misleading where the message conveyed by the indication, or any reasonable inference which could be drawn from the indication, includes any of the following:

(a) that the price is less than it in fact is;

(b) that the method for determining the price is not what it actually is;

(c) that the applicability of the price or method does not depend on the existence of facts or circumstances on which it actually does depend, for example, where the price quoted is dependent on a part exchange deal;

(d) that the price or method quoted is all inclusive when in fact there is an additional charge, for example, for postage and packaging;

(e) the price indication or method creates a false expectation that the price shown will be altered in the future, for example, where the price of the item is incorrectly indicated as an introductory offer creating an expectation that it will be increased when the introductory period is over;

(f) where the facts or circumstances upon which consumers might reasonably be expected to judge the validity of a price, or a method of determining price comparisons, are not what is indicated, for example, inaccurate price comparisons.

Does it matter how price indications are given?

The Act will apply regardless of the manner in which price indications are given. The Act has been held to apply to price indications which have been given in the following circumstances:

(a) in catalogues or brochures;

(b) in advertising of any description;

(c) in price lists;

(d) in circulars;

(e) by way of telesales;

(f) by way of oral statements made by sales people;

(g) as part of in store promotions;

(h) on price tickets;

(i) on shelf edge markers;

(j) on all other point of sale material.

How to avoid giving a misleading price indication

In order to avoid applying a misleading price indication, care should be taken to ensure that all relevant information is set out in the indication and that the information is accurate, for example:

(a) Where the price will apply for a limited period that should be made clear.

(b) The full price which the consumer will have to pay should be made clear, inclusive of VAT and other duties and any other charges, such as call out charges.

(c) Any restrictions on the offer should be mentioned, for example, if it is restricted to the first 50 customers or limited to items of a particular size or colour.

(d) It should be remembered that it is the message conveyed by the indication or the *reasonable inference* that can be drawn from it that matters for the purposes of the Act. The meaning which the advertiser or trader had in mind when they gave the indication is not determinative. Price indications should, therefore, be scrutinised to ensure that their meaning is clear. Account should be taken of any inferences which a reasonable consumer might draw.

(e) In order to ensure that the meaning is clear, the price indication should use the everyday meaning of words. Abbreviations should be avoided (with the exception of RRP (to mean recommended retail price) and 'man. rec. price' (to mean manufacturers recommended price) which are both permitted abbreviations under the Code of Practice for Traders on Price Indications.

(f) Where goods are supplied in a form which is different from the form in which they are advertised, displayed or demonstrated, the accompanying price indication should make that fact clear, for example, price indications for furniture which is purchased in kit form but displayed ready assembled should make it clear that the goods are not supplied ready assembled.

Further, and more specific, guidance can be found in the Code of Practice.

Defences to the criminal offences

There are five defences under the Act, although not all of them apply to both the offences. The defences are as follows:

(a) A publisher has a defence in respect of a misleading price indication which he publishes in an advertisement if he can demonstrate the following matters:

- he is a person who carries on the business of publishing or arranging for the publication of advertisements; and

- he received the advertisement for publication in the ordinary course of that business; and

- at the time of publication of the advertisement he did not know and had no grounds for suspecting that the publication would involve the commission of an offence. This means that the defence may not apply in circumstances where it is obvious that the price indication is misleading.

(b) Recommended prices:

It is a defence to a charge of applying a misleading price indication (but not to a charge of applying a price indication which subsequently becomes misleading) if the defendant trader can show that the indication which is applied does not relate to the availability from it of any goods or services. The defendant must also show that it has recommended a price to every person from whom the goods or services were indicated as being available and that the price indication was misleading only because of a failure to follow that indication. The defendant must also show that it was reasonable for it to assume that its recommendation would be followed.

(c) Where an indication is published in a book, newspaper, magazine, film or television programme it is a defence to show that the indication was not contained in an advertisement, for example, if it was contained in an editorial.

(d) Reasonable precautions and due diligence:

It is a defence for a person charged with the offence of applying misleading prices (but not with the offence of applying a price indication which subsequently becomes misleading) to show that he took all reasonable steps and exercised all due diligence to avoid committing the offence.

In practice, this defence is rarely made out in full. It is not sufficient to show that reasonable steps were taken to avoid liability. What must be shown is that *all* reasonable steps were taken and *all* due diligence was exercised. If the court takes the view that a step could reasonably have been taken to avoid the commission of an offence but that it was overlooked, the defence will probably not succeed.

What is reasonable and what is due diligence depends on the facts of each particular case. A relevant consideration may be the size of the business in question, for example, a large business will generally be expected to have a more extensive system for avoiding the commission of an offence than a small business (although even a small business will be expected to do all that can reasonably be required of it). Compliance with the Code of Practice for Traders on Price Indications (see below, p 92) will not in itself mean that the defence has been made out, but non-compliance with the code will make it unlikely that a trader can make out the defence.

What does the due diligence defence involve in practice?

A checking system should be established and maintained to ensure that price indications are not misleading. A written specification for the system should be drawn up and retained. Audits should be regularly carried out to ensure that the checking system is working properly. Full written reports of the audits should be prepared and retained. These steps will help to ensure that the existence of the system and its reliability can be readily demonstrated to a court if it is ever necessary to rely on the defence. Staff should be carefully briefed to follow the system.

(e) Reliance on information given by a third party:

Where an offender has relied on information given to it by a third party he will be entitled to rely on that as a defence to a charge of applying misleading prices (but not to a charge of applying a price that subsequently becomes misleading), provided that it was reasonable in all the circumstances to rely on the information, having regard in particular to the steps he took to verify the information and the steps which he might reasonably have taken to do so and whether he had any reason to disbelieve the information.

In practice, if the defence is to succeed, steps should be taken to verify information from third parties about price indications before they are applied. Such information should not simply be taken on trust.

The Code of Practice for Traders on Price Indications 1988

The Code of Practice provides practical guidance to the provisions of the Act and promotes desirable practices in the application of price indications.

The legal status of the Code

The Code is not law. The Act does not require compliance with the Code. However, a court can take into account in any prosecution whether the trader has followed the Code. If he has, whilst that will not be a complete defence, it will tend to show that no offence has been committed. Conversely, if a trader has not complied with the Code when giving a price indication, that may tend to show that the price indication is misleading. Failure to follow the Code is likely to make it difficult to satisfy the defence of due diligence (see above, p 91), although compliance with the Code will not necessarily mean that the defence will have been met.

The Code is available free of charge from the DTI.

Some specific situations covered by the Code

Comparisons with another trader's prices

A comparison with another trader's prices should only be made where the prices being compared are accurate and up to date. The Code makes no provision for the inclusion of a disclaimer or a statement of clarification to the effect that the price was correct at the time that the advertisement or promotion went to press.

The trader making the comparison should be identified clearly and prominently and, where appropriate, the shop where the other trader's price applies should be named.

The comparison should be like for like, that is, the price of the same products or of products which are substantially the same should be compared. Any differences in the products should be clearly stated.

Free offers

Where conditions are attached to a 'free offer', the main conditions should be made clear to the consumer as part of the price indication. Details of goods which consumers will have to buy before they can take advantage of the free offer will always be a main condition for these purposes.

It should also be made clear to consumers, before they are committed to purchase, where they can get a set of all the conditions from.

An offer should not be described as 'free' if additional charges have been imposed on the goods in question or the price of any product which the consumer must buy to take advantage of the offer has been inflated or will be reduced to those consumers who do not take up the offer.

Introductory offers

The term 'introductory offer' should not be used unless there is an intention to continue to offer the item in question at a higher price when the introductory period has expired.

The introductory period should not be allowed to run on so long as to make the term 'introductory offer' misleading. A reasonable length for an introductory offer period is likely to be a matter of weeks rather than months, depending on the shelf life of the product. An offer is unlikely to be misleading if the expiry date of the offer period is clearly stated on the packaging and is kept to.

References to value or worth

The code advises that references to an article's value or worth should be avoided. Where an advertisement for a watch expressed it to be 'worth £50', but offered it for sale at £4.99, the claim was held to be a misleading price indication. The court heard evidence that the watch in question was not generally available at the time that the advertisement appeared at the value indicated in the advertisement (£50). The indication was therefore misleading.

VAT

All price indications given to *consumers* should be inclusive of VAT. Price indications for business customers (for example, in advertisements for, or in shops which do most of their business with, business customers) can be shown to be VAT exclusive. However, if the trader also does business with private customers, it should be made clear that the prices indicated are VAT exclusive. In addition, VAT inclusive prices should also be displayed with the same prominence as the exclusive prices or prominent statements should be displayed stating that in addition to the price quoted, customers will have to pay VAT at the current rate.

The above is not an exhaustive treatment of the Code. There can be no substitute for reading the Code in its entirety.

CHAPTER 7

MISLEADING ADVERTISEMENTS

The Control of Misleading Advertisements Regulations 1988

The Control of Misleading Advertisements Regulations 1988 (the Regulations) SI 1988/915 apply to all advertisements with the exception of advertisements for investments and most other advertisements for financial services.

The regulations are enforced by the Director General of Fair Trading, who considers advertisements which are brought to his attention under the Regulations. Complaints can only be on the ground that an advertisement is misleading. An advertisement is *misleading* if it in any way deceives or is likely to deceive those to whom it reaches or is addressed and if, by reason of its deceptive nature, it is likely to affect their economic behaviour or, for those reasons, injures or is likely to injure a competitor of the person whose interests the advertisement seeks to promote. When deciding whether an advertisement is misleading, the way in which it is presented should be considered as well as the factual claims which it makes.

The Director General will not consider any advertisement brought to his attention under the Regulations unless the established means of dealing with the complaint have already been invoked. In practice, this will generally mean that, before contacting the Director General, complaints should be made to the appropriate industry authority, such as the Advertising Standards Authority, the Independent Television Commission, the Radio Authority, ICSTIS or to a Trading Standards Authority.

The Director General must be satisfied that the established authorities have been given a reasonable opportunity to deal with the complaint in question and that they have not dealt with it adequately. The balance is, therefore, weighted in favour of allowing the industry bodies to regulate the industry without outside interference. One of the factors to which the Regulations state that the Director General must have regard is the desirability of encouraging the control of advertisements by self-regulatory bodies.

The Advertising Standards Authority have on occasions reported advertisers to the Director General in circumstances where advertisers have refused to comply with their decisions or have persistently contravened the Committee of Advertising Practice Codes of Practice.

Consideration of complaints

The Director General must be satisfied that any complaint which is made to him is not of a frivolous or vexatious nature.

If, having considered the complaint, the Director General is of the view that the advertisement complained about is misleading and that all established methods of dealing with the complaint have been tried unsuccessfully, he may, if he thinks it appropriate, apply to the court for an injunction to restrain publication of the advertisement. The Director General is required to give reasons to support his decision whether or not to apply for an injunction. As part of the consideration process, the Director General may require the advertiser to provide to him such information as he requests to enable him to consider the advertisement fully. The court can compel compliance with the Director General's notice.

Where the Director General applies for an injunction, the court will only grant it if it agrees that the advertisement is misleading. The court can require any person who appears to bear responsibility for the appearance of the advertisement to provide evidence of the factual claims in the advertisement. If the evidence is not provided to the court, or is considered to be inaccurate, the court is entitled to find that the claims are inaccurate. Any injunction granted could extend beyond the particular advertisement which is the subject of the application to include advertisements in similar terms or which are likely to convey a similar impression.

The Director General does not have to demonstrate to the court that any person has suffered loss or damage as a result of the advertisement, nor that the advertiser intended to mislead.

Television and radio

Complaints about misleading advertisements broadcast on television (including cable services) or radio should be made to the Independent Television Commission or the Radio Authority. Complaints about advertisements broadcast on S4C should be made to the Welsh Authority. Each of these authorities has the power to require evidence to prove the accuracy of factual claims in advertisements. Failure to supply such evidence to the authority shall entitle it to make a finding that the claims are misleading. If the authority is of the opinion that the advertisement is misleading, it can direct its licensees to withdraw the advertising.

False trade descriptions and misleading prices

Trade descriptions are regulated by the Trade Descriptions Act 1968. Misleading price indications are regulated by the Consumer Protection Act 1987. Non-compliance with either piece of legislation can result in the commission of criminal offences. Readers are referred to Chapters 5 and 6 for further details.

Other causes of action in respect of misleading claims in advertisements

Misrepresentation

Misleading statements in advertisements can result in advertisers being liable to those who enter into contracts with the advertiser in reliance of those statements and who suffer loss as a result. To establish liability, the contract must be with the advertiser itself. The aggrieved party may be able to recover damages from an advertiser with whom he has contracted and/or to set the contract aside.

Deceit and negligence

Even where there is no contract in place between the advertiser and customer, the customer may in some circumstances have causes of action against the advertiser for the torts of deceit or negligence, although both of these causes of action would be difficult to pursue successfully.

Foods

The Food Safety Act 1990 makes it a criminal offence falsely to describe any foods or to make statements that are likely to mislead about its nature, substance or quality – including its nutritional or dietary value. The publisher of the advertisement or any person party to the publication can be liable.

Self-regulatory Codes

All the Codes considered in this book prohibit misleading advertisements. The provisions of each Code are dealt with in detail in Part 2 of this book.

CHAPTER 8

COMPARATIVE ADVERTISING

What is comparative advertising?

Comparative advertising is advertising which makes a comparison between the advertiser's goods or services and the goods and services of third parties. The comparison can either be a direct comparison, for example, a comparison of the advertiser's product with the product of a named competitor, or a more general comparison, for example, a description of the advertiser's products as 'Best for Value'. Both types of comparative advertising are permitted subject to the matters set out below.

Legal issues

Comparison with a named competitor or product where the competitor's brand is a registered trade mark

A registered trade mark will not be infringed if it is used to identify a third party's product, provided that the use of the trade mark is in accordance with honest practice in industrial or commercial matters (s 10(6) of the Trade Marks Act 1994).

Example

Company X manufactures and supplies batteries. Its main competitor is company Y whose batteries are sold under and by reference to the name CHARGE. CHARGE is a registered trade mark belonging to Company Y registered in respect of batteries. Company X embarks upon a comparative advertising campaign with the following comparative slogan: 'Our batteries last longer than CHARGE batteries.'

The use of the CHARGE trade mark will not infringe company Y's registration, provided that the use is honest.

What does 'honest' mean?

When deciding whether the use of the trade mark in honest, the key factor is whether members of a reasonable audience would consider it to be honest. This is an objective test. The intentions of the advertiser are not determinative. If the reasonable audience finds the advertisement to be misleading to a significant degree, the use of the trade mark will be dishonest.

Advertisements should be assessed as the reasonable audience would assess them. As a general rule this means that it would be artificial to consider the advertisement on the basis of a minute textual analysis. The reasonable audience would be more likely to take a broad approach to the interpretation of the advertisement as a whole. The key questions to ask are: what is the overall message conveyed by the advertisement, and is that message, on a fair reading, seriously misleading?

It should be borne in mind that the reasonable audience will be accustomed to the use of exaggeration in advertisements and are likely to take statements which are clearly exaggerated with a pinch of salt. The use of exaggerated statements such as 'Company X's batteries blow CHARGE batteries out of the water' would not be dishonest if the reasonable audience would not interpret them literally.

But the more detailed or specific a statement is, the more likely that it will be taken to be true. For example, if company X quoted test results in its advertisements to show that its batteries last longer than CHARGE batteries, the reasonable audience would be likely to accept the results as genuine. If the results and evidence were in fact fabricated, the advertisement would be dishonest.

The reasonable audience is likely to expect a more responsible approach by advertisers of certain types of product, for example, pharmaceutical products. Because of the nature of such products the audience are likely to apply different standards and to expect all statements in advertisements to be literally true.

An advertisement will not be dishonest simply because it emphasises the benefits of the advertiser's products without drawing attention to the corresponding advantages of its competitors' products. It will not be dishonest to poke fun at a competitor's product.

Where the advertising material consists of separate documents which are intended to be read together, for example, a mailshot consisting of a brochure and a separate leaflet, the documents should be construed together. Liability will not be avoided by including the competitor's trade mark in, say the leaflet, and the misleading information in the brochure.

The court's approach to the construction of advertisements can be very favourable to advertisers. This is illustrated by the case of *British Telecommunications plc v AT&T Communications (UK) Limited* [1997] 5 EIPR D-134. The case concerned a comparison contained in AT&T's advertising material of AT&T's rates for overseas calls as compared with those of BT. The material, which consisted of a brochure, a welcome pack and a leaflet, contained the following statement:

> On the whole our competitive rates work out cheaper per minute than BT for long distance calls in the UK and when you use our chosen country call plans, we are up to 40% cheaper on international calls.

BT is a registered trade mark belonging to British Telecom, which sued AT&T for trade mark infringement, claiming that the assertion that savings of up to 40% were available was dishonest.

The court found that BT did not have an arguable case for alleging trade mark infringement. The overall message of the advertising material was that, taken as a whole, AT&T's service promised substantial overall savings on customer's bills. BT was not able to show that this general statement was dishonest. BT's approach in isolating a particular statement from the overall advertising was misconceived. The judge did not find that the advertisements as a whole would be understood by the reasonable audience to mean savings of up to 40% could be achieved. He observed that a minute, textual analysis of the text of the advertisement would be artificial because the reasonable audience does not read advertisements in that way. The decision was also reached on the basis that the reasonable audience is used to the ways of advertisers and would therefore expect, and disregard, a certain amount of exaggeration.

It is suggested that, whilst the overall approach adopted by the court in construing advertisements is sensible, the AT&T decision falls on the wrong side of the line. It is surprising that the advertisement was not construed to have a meaning that savings of up to 40% could be achieved, when it clearly made that statement.

Misleading use of a registered trade mark

Where a registered trade mark is used in such a way in an advertisement as is likely to mislead or confuse the audience into believing that the products being compared come from the same source or are otherwise connected, the use of the trade mark is likely to be a trade mark infringement and/or a passing off (see below, p 103). Care should therefore be taken to make clear that the advertisement is a comparison of two unconnected products or businesses.

The reader is referred to Chapter 1 for further details about registered trade marks.

Trade libel/malicious falsehood

An action for trade libel or malicious falsehood will lie where statements are made in advertisements about a competitor or its products which are (a) untrue, (b) likely to cause financial loss to the competitor and (c) made by the advertiser in circumstances where the advertiser knew that the statements were untrue or did not care whether they were true or false.

In the case of *Compaq v Dell* (1992) FSR 93, Compaq objected to a comparative advertisement by rival computer manufacturer Dell. Certain statements in the advertisement were held to be false and misleading, for example, the advertisement did not compare 'like with like' in that it compared recommended retail prices with actual sales prices and some of the machines which were being compared did not share essential features. On proceedings for an interlocutory injunction, which involved Compaq demonstrating that they had an arguable case in malicious falsehood, the court granted an injunction to restrain further publication.

The burden of proving that the statement is untrue will lie on the competitor.

Where a competitor is not named in an advertisement, it can still bring an action if it can show that the advertisement would be understood by members of the audience to be a reference to it.

Example

Company X advertises its batteries with the following slogan: 'Our batteries are better than the batteries offered by our leading competitors.' Company Y, X's closest competitor, is not named in the advertisement. However, if the audience would understand the advertisement to refer to Y, Y could bring proceedings against X.

In deciding whether the advertisement or any statements contained in it are untrue, the court will determine the meaning of the statement. In doing so, it likely to adopt the same approach to construction as is set out above in relation to trade mark infringement so that it will draw out the overall meaning of the advertisement and make allowance for obvious exaggeration.

The meaning that the advertiser *intended* the advertisement to bear is irrelevant. What is important is the meaning conveyed to the audience. Care should be taken to consider all possible meanings that an advertisement might bear. If an unintended meaning were upheld by the court, the advertiser would have to defend that meaning.

Advertisers should take steps to ensure that statements contained in advertisements can be verified and, wherever possible, retain documentary proof. Documentary proof will help to prove that the statements are correct or, even where the competitor can show that they are untrue, it will go a long way to rebut an allegation of malice.

Defamation

Care should be taken to avoid making statements which are damaging to a competitor's reputation, for example, that their products are unsafe or that their workmanship is shoddy. Such statements are likely to be defamatory. To defend a claim for defamation successfully, the advertiser must invariably prove that the statements are true.

The reader is referred to the Chapter 3 for further details about defamation and trade libel.

Passing off

If the comparative advertisement does not make a clear comparison between the advertiser and the competitor, but instead confuses the public into thinking that there is a connection between the advertiser and competitor's products, for example, that they come from the same source, the advertisement could amount to a passing off. A passing off is a misrepresentation causing confusion and therefore damage to a competitor's goodwill, resulting in financial loss or the likelihood of financial loss.

Care should therefore be taken to ensure that the advertisement is clearly a comparison between unrelated companies or products.

Example of a comparative advertisement held to be a passing off

Burger King's advertisement for its Whopper burger used the phrase 'It's not just Big, Mac'. The phrase was intended to be a comparison between McDonald's Big Mac burger and Burger King's own Whopper burger. McDonald's were able to produce evidence that on seeing the advertisement some people were confused into thinking that the Big Mac and Whopper products were in some way connected and passing off was established (*McDonald's Hamburgers v Burger King (UK)* [1987] FSR 112).

Readers are referred to Chapter 2 for a more detailed treatment of the law of passing off.

Copyright infringement

Where a comparative advertisement features the distinctive elements of a competitor's product or of its advertising, those features are likely to be copyright works. The competitor may be able to rely on copyright to prevent the reproduction of its mark. The unauthorised reproduction of distinctive features such as logos, jingles, words written in stylised forms, etc, should therefore be avoided. Representations of the competitor's product or packaging might also infringe copyright, as might the reproduction of competitors' price lists or brochures.

The reader is referred to Chapter 4 for a more detailed treatment of the law of copyright.

Price comparisons

It is a criminal offence to make a misleading price comparison pursuant to the Consumer Protection Act 1987. That Act is supported by a Code of Practice, the Code of Practice for Traders on Price Indications, which provides guidance on the Act's requirements. The Code states that comparisons must be clear. The prices quoted must be accurate and up to date and the name of the other trader must be given clearly and prominently. Where the other trader is a retailer, the shop where its price applies should be given. The comparison must be in respect of the same products or products that are substantially the same, with any difference clearly stated.

The reader is referred to Chapter 6 for further detail.

The industry Codes

The advertising industry Codes (the Committee of Advertising Practice, the Independent Television Commission and the Radio Authority Codes) all contain provisions on comparative advertising.

The codes share the same essential requirements as follows:

(a) comparisons should be clear and fair;

(b) the subject of the comparison should not be selected in such a way as to confer an artificial advantage on the advertiser and must be fairly selected;

(c) like should be compared with like;

(d) points of comparison must be based on evidence that can be substantiated;

(e) the goodwill of any other business must not be used unfairly.

The approach taken by the industry authorities to the construction of advertisements tends to be stricter than that taken by the courts. They tend to require verification of each statement contained in the advertisement construed in a literal way. Set out below are examples of the ASA's approach to comparisons as an illustration of the operation of the codes in practice.

(a) Comparisons must be clear and fair.

(b) The basis of the comparison should be made clear. Comparisons should be with products on the market and not with obsolete or withdrawn products.

(c) Like should be compared with like. The elements of any comparison should not be selected in a way which gives the advertiser an artificial advantage. There has been a spate of decisions in recent times over comparisons of tariffs in the mobile telecommunications industries. The decisions emphasise that where tariffs are compared, the most comparable tariffs should be used.

Example

Objections were received to an advertisement for Mercury Communications which purported to compare the cost of a Mercury telephone call to Australia or New Zealand with that of BT. The comparison was between the Mercury Economy service (applicable at off peak times) and the BT standard rate. The ASA considered that the comparison was unfair and misleading because it did not use the most comparable BT rate. It asked the advertiser to use the most similar rate in future (*Mercury Communications Limited – ASA Monthly Report No 76, September 1997*).

Objections were received to an advertisement comparing Worldcom charges with those of Mercury. The advertisement featured a chart showing a comparison of tariffs offered by the two businesses. The Mercury tariff was described simply as the Mercury tariff. It was not named or otherwise particularised. Mercury complained that the tariff featured was not in fact the tariff that was most comparable with the advertiser's service.

The complaint was upheld on similar grounds to the BT case above. The ASA also upheld the complaint that the comparison was unclear in that it did not give details of the Mercury tariff relied on (*Worldcom – ASA Monthly Report No 76, September 1997*).

It is therefore important that the advertiser does its homework before making comparisons to ensure that like is really compared with like.

Where prices are compared, they must be up to date. The Code will be contravened where an out of date price is used. This will be the case even where a disclaimer is included to state that the comparison was correct at a certain date.

(d) Advertisers must not *unfairly* attack or denigrate other businesses or their products when making comparisons.

Example

BT objected to a poster using the headlines 'BRITISH TELECON THE GREAT PHONE ROBBERY ... DON'T WASTE MONEY SWITCH TO CABLE'.

The complaint was that the advertisements unfairly denigrated BT by insinuating that it was dishonest and was duping the public by charging inflated prices. The complaint was upheld on the basis that it was an unfair denigration of BT (*Bell Cablemedia – ASA Monthly Report No 73, June 1997*).

(e) The products of another business should never be shown as broken or defaced *unless* the effect is used to illustrate comparative tests. Even then the details of the tests should be made clear.

(f) Comparative advertisements must comply with the rule relating to truthfulness. Advertisers should hold evidence to prove that the claims which are made in the comparison are true. The reader is referred to Chapter 17 for guidance about the ASA's approach to the interpretation of factual claims in advertisements. An example of the approach in relation to a comparative advertisement concerns an advertisement for the NordicTrack skier. The advertisement stated that the skier burnt more calories than other exercise machines and that unlike bikes, treadmills and step machines the NordicTrack skier exercised all the muscles in the body.

The complainants challenged the claims and alleged that they were misleading. Their complaints were upheld. The advertisers did not produce evidence to prove that the NordicTrack skier exercised *all* muscles as claimed in the advertisement (although the advertisers could demonstrate that it worked the upper and lower body). Similarly, the advertisers could not prove that the NordicTrack skier burnt more calories, although they had produced reports of studies carried out by research institutions (*NordicTrack (UK) Limited – ASA Monthly Report No 74, July 1997*).

Comparisons should be up to date

Legal issues

Price comparisons are required to be up to date at the time of use by the Code of Practice for Traders on Price Comparisons. It is unlikely that an advertiser could safeguard its position from last minute price changes by competitors by inserting a suitably worded and prominent rider to the effect that prices were correct as at, for example, the date of going to press. Whilst a rider may have that effect, and the writer recommends that such a rider always be used when making price comparisons, such a statement may not be a complete defence. It is recommended that advertisers liaise with their local trading standards departments if in any doubt about the accuracy of a price comparison.

As regards other comparisons, care should be taken to ensure that comparisons are up to date. If they are not, there is a risk that the advertisement may be found to be dishonest (and therefore a potential trade mark infringement or trade libel). As with price comparisons, advertisers are advised that that a suitably worded and prominent rider that the information is up to date as at, for example, the date of publication, should be included in advertisements.

The Codes

Comparisons should be up to date at the time that advertisements are actually *used*. It is insufficient, at least for the purposes of the ASA, to insert a statement of clarification that the comparison was correct at an earlier date.

The European Directive on Comparative Advertising

The European Commission has finalised a Directive which will regulate comparative advertising across the European Union.[1] It is intended to harmonise the laws on comparative advertising throughout the EU, although the Directive is not clear as to whether it is a harmonisation measure or whether it simply lays down the *minimum* legal requirements throughout the EU. The Directive is set to be incorporated into UK law in the year 2000. The Directive must come into force not later than April 2000.

The Directive is likely to be incorporated into UK law by way of amendment to the Control of Misleading Advertisements Regulations 1988 (the reader is referred to Chapter 7 for consideration of the provisions of these regulations). The effect of this method of incorporation will be to deny complainants the right to direct access to the courts if there is a breach of the Directive's provisions. Instead, the complainant must exhaust all alternative avenues of complaint, for example, by complaining to the Advertising Standards Authority or the Independent Television Commission or the Radio Authority. If those authorities do not deal with the complaints adequately, recourse can then be made to the Director General of Fair Trading who is empowered to apply to the court to obtain an injunction to restrain the publication of the offending advertisement where he believes that it is appropriate to do so.

The delegation of 'front line responsibility' for the regulation of comparative advertisements to the self-regulatory authorities is likely to mean that most comparative advertisements will be judged according to the strict method of interpreting advertisements, which is favoured by the authorities. In practice it is therefore likely to be more difficult to engage in comparative advertising than at present.

The terms of the Directive

The Directive makes clear that comparative advertising is permissible throughout the European Union provided it complies with the conditions which it sets out. The most significant of these are as follows:

(a) The comparison must not be misleading.

(b) The comparison must not discredit or denigrate the branding of the competitor.

(c) The comparison must not take unfair advantage of the reputation or the branding or other distinguishing features of the competitor's products.

---

[1]   Directive 97/55, amending Directive 84/450.

(d) The comparison must objectively compare one or more material, relevant and representative features of the products.

(e) Like must be compared with like.

(f) The comparison must not create confusion in the marketplace between the advertiser and a competitor, or between the advertiser's trade marks, trade names, other distinguishing marks, goods or services and those of a competitor.

(g) The comparison must not present goods or services as imitations or replicas of goods or services bearing a protected trade mark or trade name.

The workings of the Directive, when implemented into UK law, are a matter of some debate. Practitioners are advised to consult their legal representatives at the time of its implementation. For a detailed analysis of its likely effects. The reader is also referred to Chapter 16 of this book.

CHAPTER 9

COMPETITIONS

Competitions are a popular form of sales promotion, but they involve serious legal risks. Care must be taken to ensure that a competition does not take the form of a lottery.

Subject to very limited exceptions (for example, the National Lottery), lotteries are illegal pursuant to the Lotteries and Amusements Act 1976 (the Act). This Act does not apply to Northern Ireland. It is a *criminal offence* to conduct an illegal lottery.

What is a lottery?

'Lottery' is a term of art which is broader than most people would expect.

The term lottery has been defined as the distribution of prizes by chance where the participants, or a substantial number of them, make a payment or other consideration in return for obtaining the chance to win a prize (*Reader's Digest Association Limited v Williams* [1976] 3 All ER 737).

The definition breaks down into three elements as follows:

(a) the distribution of *prizes;*

(b) which must be *by chance;*

(c) in circumstances where a *contribution* is made by participants in return for the chance of winning a prize.

If one of these elements is removed, a promotion will not be a lottery.

Example of an illegal lottery

Packets of tea were produced containing a coupon which informed purchasers that they had won a named prize. It was only after opening the packet that the purchaser knew what the prize was.

This promotion was illegal for the following reasons:

(a) it involved a distribution of prizes;

(b) which depended on chance; and

(c) by purchasing the tea, the consumer was making a payment for the chance of winning a particular prize (*Taylor v Smeton* (1883) 11 QBD 207).

It is the substance of the promotion which is important, and not the label that is applied to it.

How to ensure that a promotion is not an illegal lottery

The creation of an illegal lottery will be avoided if *any one* of the three elements set out above is removed.

Ensuring that prizes are not distributed by chance

To ensure that prizes are not distributed by chance, the promotion must involve participants in the exercise of skill or judgment. The degree and type of skill or judgment which is required must meet the legal requirements.

Degree of skill

Section 14 of the Act makes it an offence for any person to conduct in the course of a trade or business a competition in which success does not depend *to a substantial degree* on the exercise of skill. No guidance about the degree of skill which is necessary to satisfy this criterion is given.

Type of skill

The Act contains restrictions on certain types of skill as follows:

(a) Where prizes are offered for the forecast of a future event the competition will be unlawful.

(b) Where prizes are offered for the forecast of a past event where the result is not yet ascertained or is not widely known the competition will be unlawful.

What is 'skill'?

The Act does not define what is meant by skill. Each competition must be judged on its own merits.

Competitions which involve questions will generally involve skill and judgment. However if a very obvious question is asked (for example, what is the name of the day that follows Monday?), it will risk falling foul of the legal requirements on the ground that the degree of skill required to answer the question is insufficient.

Competitions which involve puzzles, multiple choice type questions or the exercise of judgment (for example, 'arrange the following criteria in order of importance …') will generally involve sufficient skill, as will competitions which involve originality (for example, 'devise a slogan in *x* words').

Two-stage promotions

Competitions sometimes have two stages. It is important that neither stage is determined by chance. Success must depend to a substantial degree on the exercise of skill at each stage of the promotion. If any part of a promotion involves a lottery the whole promotion will become unlawful.

Example of an illegal two-stage promotion

Tins of cat food were sold bearing labels on the inside of which were a bingo card and a line of numbers. If the numbers matched the numbers on the bingo card, the consumer was entitled to a prize. In order to claim the prize, the contestant had to solve an accompanying puzzle involving an element of skill.

It was held that the scheme was in two stages. The first was the chance of finding a label with numbers that matched the numbers on the card. This stage was determined entirely by chance. The second stage was the puzzle and involved skill. No skill was required by the first stage. The inclusion of an element of skill in stage two was not sufficient to prevent the scheme being an illegal lottery (*DPP v Bradfute Associates Limited* [1967] 2 QB 291).

The selection of prizewinners

The way that prizewinners are chosen must not be dependent on chance. If a tiebreaker decides the winner, it will probably be legal. But if the prizewinner is chosen at random, for example, where the winning answer is pulled out of a hat, it is likely to be illegal.

Removal of the requirement for contribution

In order to remove the requirement for contribution, a promotion has to be free of *any charge whatsoever* to at least a substantial number of participants. It is not sufficient that the entry into the promotion does not involve an *extra* charge over and above the usual purchase price of the goods in question.

In the case of *Imperial Tobacco v HM Attorney General* [1981] AC 718, packets of cigarettes were sold containing scratchcards which featured cash prizes. The packets containing the cards were distinguishable from packets which did not have cards. The packs with cards retailed at the same price as the packs without.

It was held that the promotion was an illegal lottery. It involved a payment for the chance to win a prize; namely the price of the cigarettes. It was immaterial that no part of the purchase price could be allocated to the chance to win a prize.

A good working test to adopt is whether entry into the competition is conditional on any type of cost to the participant. Is there a hidden entry fee, such as the cost of a premium rate telephone call? If so, warning bells should start to ring alerting all concerned to the possibility that the promotion may be an illegal lottery.

Alternative methods of entry

The creation of an illegal lottery can be avoided by offering participants an alternative way of taking part which does not involve any cost.

In the case of *Express Newspapers v Liverpool Daily Post* [1985] 1 WLR 1089, a newspaper bingo game was held not to be dependent on payment. Copies of the newspaper, and therefore of the bingo numbers, were available free of charge from a number of sources which were not dependent on a purchase of the newspaper. The numbers could also be obtained by ringing the newspaper.

The Crown Prosecution Service has issued a policy statement concerning alternative methods of entry. The statement indicates that:

(a) It is not in itself sufficient to make a scheme lawful that some participants do not have to purchase a chance in the draw.

(b) The position is likely to be different where there is a genuine, realistic and unlimited alternative method of entry which is free.

How to ensure that the alternative entry method is genuine, realistic and unlimited

Information about the existence of the alternative method of entry should be available to potential participants before they make a decision to purchase. It is usual to state that no purchase of the relevant goods is necessary. This statement should appear on all promotional or advertising material relating to the competition, in the rules of the competition itself and on all packs of the products to which the promotion relates. The statement should be sufficiently prominent to come to the attention of purchasers without their having to scrutinise the small print.

Where prizes are awarded by means of something that is found within the product packaging, for example, in coupons enclosed in packets of crisps, the alternative entry procedure should give contestants the opportunity to send away for the means of entry free of charge.

Only one of the elements which make up a lottery has to be removed in order to avoid the creation of an illegal lottery. A competition which depends on chance, such as a prize draw or a scratchcard promotion, will not be illegal if entry to the competition is free. On the other hand, an entry charge can be levied for competitions involving skill. The introduction of the requirement for skill will avoid the creation of an illegal lottery.

The criminal offences relating to lotteries

If the promoter of an illegal lottery or any party which is directly involved in running an illegal lottery does any of the activities set out below, it will have committed a criminal offence. The offences are punishable by imprisonment and/or fines. The activities giving rise to criminal liability are as follows:

(a) Printing tickets for use in the lottery. 'Tickets' include any documents which are evidence of participation in a lottery and will include entry forms or scratchcards, for example.

(b) Selling or distributing or offering or advertising for sale or distributing any tickets or chances in the lottery.

(c) Possessing tickets or chances in the lottery for the purpose of publication or distribution.

(d) Bringing or inviting any person to send into Great Britain any ticket in or advertisement of the lottery for the purpose of sale or distribution.

(e) Sending out of Great Britain, or attempting to do so, the proceeds of sale of any ticket or chance in the lottery or any document recording such sale or distribution or the identities of the holders of the tickets/ chances.

(f) Printing, publishing or distributing or possessing for the purpose of doing so:

- an advertisement for the lottery;
- a list of prize winners or of winning tickets in the lottery;
- any document descriptive of the drawing of the lottery which is calculated to induce people to enter.

(g) Using any premises or causing or knowingly permitting any premises to be used for purposes connected with the promotion or conduct of the lottery.

(h) Causing, procuring or attempting to procure any person to do any of the above acts.

Liability does not depend on the intention of the promoter. Lotteries can be created inadvertently.

Who can be liable?

The company whose goods are the subjects of the promotion will usually be liable as the *publisher* of the promotion. A *third party handling house* may also be liable if it is engaged in activities which are caught by the above provisions.

In theory, *printers* and *retailers* will also be guilty of a criminal offence if they engage in the above activities. In practice, the authorities will be more likely to direct their attention to the publisher of the promotion.

The CAP Codes of Advertising and Sales Promotions contain provisions which regulate competitions. They are set out in Chapter 17.

CHAPTER 10

USING PEOPLE IN ADVERTISING AND PROMOTIONS

Under UK law, there is no one specific 'personality right' which gives people the right to prevent the commercial exploitation of their name or image. It is permissible to use people, characters and personalities in advertising and promotions, except to the extent that use is prohibited by intellectual property or defamation law.

On the other hand, the industry Codes of Practice (the CAP Code, the ITC Code and the Radio Authority Code) all contain restrictions on the unauthorised use of people in advertisements. In many respects, it is the Codes which govern the effective position on the use of personalities for practical purposes.

THE LEGAL RESTRICTIONS

Defamation

The law of defamation protects *reputation*. Statements will be defamatory if they tend to make ordinary people think less of the subject of the statement. In order to bring a successful action for defamation, a personality would have to show that the use or reference to them in advertising or promotional material has caused damage to their reputation. A defamation claim of this type generally involves an allegation that the advertisement portrays the plaintiff as a hypocrite, as someone who is acting in breach of contract or of rules of professional conduct or as someone who has otherwise misled the public.

In the case of *Tolley v Fry* [1931] AC 333, the plaintiff was a well known amateur golfer. He was caricatured in an advertisement for Fry's chocolate in such a way as suggested that he was endorsing the product. Mr Tolley had not given permission for his likeness to be used in the advertisement. He commenced proceedings on the basis that the advertisement was defamatory, in that it suggested that he had agreed to advertise the product in return for payment. He alleged that this was damaging to his credit and reputation as an amateur golfer. The court upheld the claim. The advertisement clearly inferred that Mr Tolley was a hypocrite when he professed to be an amateur golfer.

Care should be taken when making unauthorised use of a personality who is known to have an exclusive merchandising contract or an employment contract which forbids him or her to participate in advertising. The unauthorised use of their name and/or likeness in promotional material could be defamatory if the personality is able to prove that *some* of the audience would have believed that he/she had agreed to appear in the advertisement in breach of contract.

The estates of dead people cannot bring proceedings for defamation.

How to avoid defamation claims

The fact that the publisher of the defamatory material did not intend to make a defamatory statement is irrelevant to liability. It is therefore important to analyse an advertisement to pick up on any unintended meanings which the advertisement might bear.

Most of the defamatory meanings which are likely to arise in connection with the unauthorised use of a personality will involve meanings that are not apparent from the face of the advertisement. The advertisement in *Tolley v Fry* would not have had a defamatory meaning unless the audience was aware of Mr Tolley's amateur status.

This type of 'hidden' meaning is known as an *innuendo*. Care should be taken to assess an advertisement for any innuendo meanings. This exercise will involve an appreciation of the public stance of the personality in question on relevant issues, for example, to ensure that a committed animal rights activist is not shown to be advertising animal fur or a known teetotaller is not used to promote alcohol. Both of these scenarios would involve an inference that the personality in question is a hypocrite by suggesting they would disregard their publicly expressed opinions for the sake of personal gain.

The use of photographs

A limited right of privacy

A person who commissions photographs (or videotapes and films or stills from them) for private or domestic purposes has the right to prevent the unauthorised publication of the material (s 85(1) of the Copyright, Designs and Patents Act 1988). The right applies to material which is commissioned for private or domestic purposes. It will not apply to uncommissioned material which happened to be taken on a private occasion, for example, photographs taken by the paparazzi. The right is owned by the *commissioner* of the material and cannot be assigned. The person who commissions the material may not be the actual subject of the photograph or film.

How to avoid infringement of the right of privacy

Care should be taken to ascertain that images which advertisers wish to use were not originally commissioned for private or domestic purposes.

Copyright in photographs

Copyright subsists in photographs. The unauthorised use of a photograph will infringe copyright in the photograph. In order to avoid infringement, the copyright owner must consent to the use of the photograph or the advertiser must acquire copyright in the photograph.

Copyright in photographs, whether commissioned or not, will belong to the *photographer* unless it has been assigned to a third party. The subject of the photograph will not own copyright unless it has been assigned to him/her. Unless the subject of the photograph has acquired copyright in the picture, he/she will have no right to restrain the publication of the photograph on the ground that it is an infringement of copyright.

Copyright in photographs expires 70 years from the death of the photographer.

How to avoid infringement

Before any photograph is used, the advertiser should check whether copyright in the photograph has expired and, if it has not, a licence should be obtained from the copyright owner. Alternatively, the advertiser should acquire copyright by way of an assignment from the copyright owner.

Photographs taken from stills of films

Unauthorised use of a still will be an infringement of copyright in the film from which it was taken. A licence should therefore be obtained from the copyright owners, who will usually be the production company and the principal director, or sometimes just the production company. The copyright owner will not necessarily be the individual(s) who are shown in the still.

Copyright in films expires 70 years from the death of the death of the last of certain named individuals, details of which are set out in Chapter 4.

How to avoid infringement of copyright

A licence should be obtained from the copyright owner.

Will photographs which are taken from stills infringe performance rights?

A performer has the right to prevent the unauthorised commercial exploitation of the recording of their performance. This right is a relatively recent introduction to the law. So far as the author is aware, a UK court has not had to consider whether the use of a single still which features a performer could be said to constitute an infringement of that performer's rights. In the author's opinion, a still is *capable* of infringing a performer's rights. In order to err on the side of caution, consent should be sought from the owner of the performance rights. This may not be the performer. The rights can, and often are assigned, usually to the film production company.

Performance rights last for 50 years from the end of the calendar year in which the performance took place if a recording of the performance is released during that period or, if not, 50 years from the end of the year of release.

How to avoid infringement of performance rights

Obtain a licence from the rights owner.

Use of film footage or soundtracks

The above observations apply equally to the use of footage as to the use of stills. A licence to use the footage or soundtrack will be required from the copyright owner. Performance rights should also be cleared.

Copyright in signatures

An individual's signature may be an artistic work protected under copyright law. If so, the unauthorised reproduction of the signature will infringe copyright. The name itself will *not* be protected by copyright. It is the *appearance* of the signature which may be protected. It should be remembered that copyright subsists in works which are the product of skill, judgment and labour. An everyday signature of a rudimentary nature is unlikely to meet this test. The more elaborate the signature, the more likely that it will be protected by copyright.

How to avoid infringement

Assess whether the signature is capable of being a copyright work. If there is a risk that it is protected by copyright then permission to use the signature should be obtained from the copyright owner (who will almost certainly be the author of the signature).

Copyright in a name

It is well established under copyright law that copyright does not exist in a person's name.

Copyright in appearance

There is no copyright in a person's appearance even if that person has a carefully crafted image, such as an elaborately made-up face. This was illustrated by the case of *Corporation of America v Harpbond* [1983] FSR 32. The case concerned the unauthorised reproduction of the pop star Adam Ant's distinctively made-up face. The court found that no copyright existed in Adam Ant's appearance.

Passing off

Can the law of passing off offer personalties the right to restrain the use of their name or appearance?

Passing off consists of the following elements:

(a) a misrepresentation

(b) made in the course of a business

(c) to prospective or actual customers

(d) which is likely to cause damage to goodwill, and

(e) which causes loss or is likely to do so.

Traditionally, the courts have resisted extending the law of passing off to restrain the unauthorised exploitation of a person's identity, likeness or image. The reluctance has been justified on the ground that the individuals who have tried to sue in passing off have been unable to establish the necessary goodwill (meaning trading reputation) in the goods or services in respect of which their image has been used.

Example

In the case of *Lyngstad v Anabas Products* [1977] FSR 62, the court refused relief to members of the pop group ABBA who sought to restrain the reproduction of their images on certain types of goods. The court found that there was no common field of activity shared by the pop group and the producers of the products. The group members were not therefore able to show that they had acquired a reputation in the merchandise in question which would be damaged by the defendants' activities. The judge observed as follows:

> Essentially what the plaintiff complains of here is not that there is a possibility of confusion between the defendants' business activities and their activities as singers, but that their activities as singers have generated a public interest which has enabled the defendants to exploit for their own purposes the use of the plaintiff's photographs and names.

The *ABBA* case, and other similar cases, can be criticised on the ground that the courts did not recognise that well known personalities often have business activities which run parallel to the areas with which they are primarily associated. These business activities extend to the licensing of their name and likeness for product endorsement and to other merchandising activities. If the court had had regard to ABBA's merchandising activities, it would have been more likely to find that a common field of activity existed between ABBA and the defendant.

A more recent case seemed to demonstrate a shift in the court's attitude towards recognition of the goodwill generated by merchandising activities. The decision was reached on an interlocutory basis (which means that the plaintiff only had to show that it had an arguable case). The case concerned the unauthorised reproduction of pictures of the Teenage Mutant Ninja Turtles on items of clothing (*Mirage Studios v Counter-Feat Clothing Company Limited* [1991] FSR 145). The owners of the rights to the image of the turtles commenced proceedings in passing off.

The court found that an arguable case of passing off was made out in the light of evidence which was produced to show the following matters:

(a) there was active licensing of the merchandising rights to the name and likeness of the Turtles;

(b) there was a connection in the public mind between the Turtles and the products bearing their likeness;

(c) a substantial number of people knew of and wished to acquire the product bearing the likeness of the Turtles.

On the basis of the evidence before it, the court found that there was a misrepresentation that the turtle figures were being reproduced by the defendant under licence from the rights owners. The court recognised that character merchandising was a common and recognised activity. At the time of the judgment, it was widely thought that, wherever the three factors set out above were present, a case might succeed in passing off.

However, in very recent cases the courts have shown a tendency to disregard the *Ninja Turtles* case and to limit the scope of passing off. A 1997 case involved unauthorised pop merchandise featuring the likeness of members of the pop group, the Spice Girls. The court said that the group was unable to demonstrate even an arguable case in passing off against Panini SpA, which was supplying an unauthorised sticker collection featuring the group. Using much the same type of arguments which had been successful in the *Turtles* case, the group argued that the reproduction of their images on Panini's product amounted to a misrepresentation that the Spice Girls had authorised the sticker collection. This argument did not find favour with the court, which held that in the absence of special circumstances the public would not be misled into buying Panini's product on the assumption that it was authorised by the group. The judge also queried whether the source of the product would be of concern to the public who would be more interested in buying a product which featured the image of their heroes (or heroines) than from where it originated (*Halliwell and Others v Panini* (Unreported, 6 June 1997)).

Both the Turtles and the Spice Girls cases concerned *character merchandising*. A claim in passing off is unlikely to be successful where character merchandising is involved unless it can be shown on the special facts of any case that the public are likely to be deceived by the use of the plaintiff's name or likeness into believing that there is a connection between the plaintiff and the goods. Specific evidence will be required to support such a claim. Reliance on the fact that the use of merchandising agreements is now commonplace is unlikely in itself to be sufficient.

The court has not defined what type of 'special facts' will give rise to a connection in the mind of the public between the celebrity and the defendant/defendant's products. One such fact is likely to be a misrepresentation that the celebrity *endorses* the defendant's product. If Panini had promoted their sticker album by representing that it had been approved by the Spice Girls, that would have been a misrepresentation that the album was connected with the group. A claim in passing off would therefore have been more likely to succeed.

Advertisements

Where advertisements make an express or an implied representation that a celebrity endorses a product or service, the representation has the potential to amount to a passing off. It could deceive the public into thinking that the product is connected with the celebrity. However, the mere use of a name or likeness without any impression of endorsement is unlikely to amount to passing off as the law currently stands.

Goodwill

In order to succeed in a passing off action, an individual would have to prove that they own goodwill in the commercial exploitation of their likeness/name which will be damaged by the misrepresentation. The wider their merchandising activity, the easier it will be for them to establish the existence of goodwill. For this reason, individuals who do not have a high public profile will find it difficult to bring a successful claim for passing off.

Damage to goodwill

The individual must also prove that the misrepresentation has caused damage to his/her goodwill or is likely to do so. Damage will generally be of two types. First, the individual may find it more difficult to secure merchandising contracts if they are perceived as having already endorsed products, especially products of the same type. There will therefore be a loss of opportunity. Secondly, the individual will have no control over the quality of the goods/services which they have been represented as promoting or endorsing. If they are of poor quality it will reflect badly on the individual.

Trade mark infringement

The name, signature and likeness of an individual can be registered as trade marks. By way of example, Alan Shearer, Paul Gascoigne and Damon Hill have all registered their names as trade marks.

Avoiding infringement

In order to avoid infringing an individual's trade mark, a search should be carried out at the Trade Mark Registry to ensure that there are no relevant trade mark registrations. In some circumstances trade marks can be infringed even if though the trade mark registrations do not cover the goods or services which are being advertised – the reader is referred to Chapter 1 for further details.

Recent legal developments are likely to make it more difficult for well known personalities to secure trade mark registrations for their names and images. The developments may also make existing registrations vulnerable to removal from the register.

In order to register a name, likeness, etc, as a trade mark it is not sufficient to show that a name, likeness or signature is well known and that it is associated with a personality. What must also be shown is that the public associates the name, etc, as a badge of origin for the goods or services for which registration is sought. If the mark is seen by the public as no more than a depiction of the personality it will *not* be sufficient to secure a trade mark registration. The mark must be distinctive, in that it enables the public to distinguish the trade mark owner's goods or services from identical or similar goods marketed by other parties.

Example

Elvis Presley Enterprises, the official merchandising company for Elvis Presley memorabilia, applied to register three trade marks as follows: ELVIS, ELVIS PRESLEY and ELVIS A PRESLEY (the latter as a signature). The application was rejected because the applicant was unable to provide evidence that the public saw the Elvis marks as anything other than a depiction of the Elvis character. In particular, no evidence was adduced to show that the marks served to distinguish the applicant's goods from goods that were not (*Re applications by Elvis Presley Enterprises Inc* (1997) *The Times*, 25 March.

Privacy

The present position

UK law does not recognise a right to privacy. The situation is to be contrasted with the position in other jurisdictions, most notably USA, Australia, Canada, France and Germany where a personality right exists.

Likely future developments

The European Convention on Human Rights (ECHR) is set to be incorporated into UK law in the relatively near future. The ECHR grants a right to respect for privacy. It remains to be seen whether the scope of the right to respect for privacy will be extended by the courts to include a right to control the use to which a person's image/personality is put for commercial purposes and, if so what form that right will take.

In theory, the incorporation of the ECHR into UK law may provide personalities with a powerful tool to carve out a *de facto* personality right.

Trade Descriptions Act 1969

It is a *criminal* offence under the Trade Descriptions Act 1968 (the Act) to give a false indication, direct or indirect, that goods and services are of a kind supplied to any person, for example, a well known personality (s 13 of the Act).

It is also an offence to make false representations as to royal approval or award in relation to goods or services (s 12 of the Act).

THE CODES OF PRACTICE

The CAP Codes

Protection of privacy – the portrayal of or referral to individuals

The CAP Codes govern the use of individuals in advertisements and sales promotions to which the Codes apply. The reader is referred to Chapter 17 for details of matters to which the Codes apply.

Advertisers are urged to obtain permission in advance if they wish to portray or refer to individuals in advertisements. The requirement applies to any individual whether or not he/she is a public figure.

'Urged' is not defined in the Code. In essence, it means that there must be a good reason for a failure to obtain permission. A permissible exception to the general rule has been held to be where a photograph depicted a crowd scene and the participants were not so well known that the advertiser could be expected to try to contact them before publication (*Halifax Building Society – ASA Monthly Report No 77, October 1997*).

Prior permission may not be needed under the Codes when the advertisement does not contain anything that is inconsistent with the position or views of the person featured.

It is also unnecessary to obtain permission where the product being advertised is a book or a film and the individual who is referred to in the advertisement is the subject of the book or film.

Care should be taken when portraying or referring to dead people to avoid causing offence or distress.

Where the individual who is portrayed or referred to without prior permission has a high public profile, and specifically where he/she is an entertainer, a politician or a sports person, a further restriction applies. Advertisers should ensure that such persons are not portrayed in an offensive or adverse way.

Example of an adverse and offensive portrayal

An example of an adverse and offensive portrayal occurred when, as part of the 1997 election campaign, the Conservative Party used a national press advertisement that featured a photograph of the leader of the Labour party, Tony Blair. In place of Mr Blair's eyes, the poster featured demonic-looking eyes. The advertisement featured the caption 'NEW LABOUR NEW DANGER'.

Complaints were received alleging that the advertisement portrayed Tony Blair, who had not given his permission for the use of his photograph, in an offensive way.

The ASA upheld the complaints. It considered that the advertisement depicted Tony Blair as a sinister and dishonest figure and that this amounted to an adverse or offensive portrayal of Mr Blair.

The injection of humour may make an otherwise offensive or adverse portrayal of a public figure acceptable. For example, during the run-up to the 1997 election, press advertisements for the satirical magazine *Private Eye* featured two previous covers of the magazine. The first featured a photograph of Michael Howard, the then Home Secretary. Below the heading appeared the words 'LUNATIC. The Eye says if we are wrong let him sue us'.

The second cover featured a photograph of the then Prime Minister, John Major, below a headline stating 'MAJOR: SHOCK WARNING' and a speech bubble from Mr Major's mouth which contained the words 'if you don't vote Conservative, Labour will get in'.

Complaints were received that the advertisements portrayed Mr Howard and Mr Major in an offensive way. The complaints were not upheld. The ASA concluded that the advertisements would be seen as humorous, especially in the context of the run-up to an election (*Pressdram limited t/a Private Eye – ASA Monthly Report No 75, August 1997*)

The Code states that advertisers must not imply an endorsement of a product or service by people with a high public profile where none exists. This requirement would apply equally to alleged endorsements by a people that do not have a high profile. Such misleading endorsements would be a breach of the rule concerning truthfulness (see Chapter 17 for further detail) as well as the rules on testimonials and endorsements.

What constitutes an endorsement?

The mere appearance of a public figure in relation to a product will not necessarily be an endorsement. Each advertisement must be considered on its own merits.

Example

Complaints were received about a national press advertisement which appeared just after the Labour victory in the 1997 general election. It advertised Holsten Pils and featured a photograph of Tony and Cherie Blair retouched to show Mrs Blair holding a bottle of lager to her lips. A caption stating 'ALL CHANGE THEN DARLING' appeared next to Mr Blair. Next to Mrs Blair were the words 'YES DEAR, SMOOTHER, CLEANER AND SURPRISINGLY EASY TO DRINK'. The complainants objected to the implication that Mr and Mrs Blair endorsed Holsten Pils.

The complaint was rejected. The ASA considered that the advertisement would be interpreted as humorous rather than as a serious endorsement and that the approach was acceptable. The published adjudication suggests that the ASA were influenced by the fact that the advertisement was a one off and was not intended to appear again. If the advertisement was part of a sustained campaign the decision may have been different.

References to the royal family

References to members of the royal family or to the royal arms and emblems are not permitted under the Code without consent from the Lord Chamberlain's office. The use of royal warrants should be cleared with the Royal Warrant Holders' Association.

The ITC Code

The ITC Code provides that individual living persons must neither be portrayed or referred to in advertisements without their permission having first been obtained except where the ITC has approved the advertisement. Portrayal extends to impersonations (including impersonations of well known voices), parodies and caricatures.

Permission is required even where an individual is referred to indirectly, provided the reference enables the viewer to clearly identify him/her.

There is an exception to the rule for prior permission in relation to advertisements for books, films, particular editions of TV or radio programmes, newspapers, magazines, etc, which feature the person referred to in the advertisement, provided that the reference or portrayal is neither offensive or defamatory.

In the case of generic advertising for news media, ITC licensees may waive the requirement for prior permission if it seems reasonable to expect that the individual concerned would not have reason to object. However, such generic advertising should be immediately withdrawn if individuals who are portrayed without their permission object.

The Radio Authority Code

The Radio Authority code states that individual living persons must not normally be portrayed or referred to in advertisements without their prior permission.

Similar exceptions to those contained in the ITC Code exist in relation to advertisements for books, films, radio and television programmes, newspapers, magazines, etc, and generic news media advertising.

The Code advises that advance permission be obtained where impersonations or soundalikes of well known characters are to be used.

References to, and portrayals of, people who are active in politics should be carefully worded to avoid falling foul of the rules which require that political matters should be treated impartially and that advertisements must not be directed towards any political end.

CHAPTER 11

THE PROTECTION OF FORMATS IN ADVERTISEMENTS AND SALES PROMOTIONS

The 'format' of an advertisement, an advertising campaign or a promotion is the underlying features which exist in relation to each type of promotion. These could include particular themes or characters. It is not uncommon for advertisers to complain that competitors have copied their format or for agencies who have been involved in pitches for new business to find that the ideas which they presented have been used by the client, even though the business went to a different agency. This chapter examines the extent to which the law provides protection against the copying of formats.

Copyright protection

Copyright gives the copyright owner the right to prevent the unauthorised reproduction of his/her original artistic, literary, musical or dramatic works. To benefit from copyright protection, the work must be original. This term is explained in Chapter 4. The work must also have been developed to an extent where it has been set down in writing, or in another material form, and is capable of being realised. Very woolly ideas expressed in an abstract way are unlikely to benefit from protection under copyright law.

Copyright works

In order to bring a claim for copyright infringement, it must first be shown that copyright subsists in the work for which protection is sought.

Written material and music

Copyright will exist in original proposals, scripts, copy, artistic material (for example, storyboards) or music (for example, jingles). It will enable the owner of copyright to prevent the copying of a substantial part of the protected works. As discussed above, the material for which copyright protection is sought must be more detailed than the expression of general ideas or concepts. The more novel the idea or the more detailed the script, the easier it will be to establish that copyright subsists in it. Material should therefore be expressed in as much detail as possible. Titles and slogans are unlikely to attract copyright protection, because they are generally considered to be too trite to be deserving of it (see Chapter 4 for further detail). They can, however, often be protected by trade mark registrations.

Copyright in the above materials is unlikely to extend to the underlying ideas contained in them. It protects the way in which the concepts have been used. Other parties may use the underlying concepts in different ways. In such circumstances copyright is unlikely to provide any redress.

Dramatic format

Copyright may subsist in the dramatic format of advertisements which are broadcast on television or radio. It will, however, be difficult to establish ownership of copyright in formats as opposed to scripts or other detailed material.

This is demonstrated by the case of *Green v Broadcasting Corporation of New Zealand* [1989] 2 All ER 1056. In that case, the plaintiff sought to restrain the defendant from broadcasting a television programme which was similar to the plaintiff's Opportunity Knocks show. Opportunity Knocks was essentially a talent show which was presented in a particular manner incorporating certain original features. The plaintiff relied on copyright in the 'dramatic format' of the show. The dramatic format on which he based his case was not the overall show, but the distinctive features which were repeated in each programme. These consisted of the programme title, the use of certain catch phrases and the use of a device known as a clapometer which measured audience reaction to competitors' performances.

The court held that it was stretching the notion of dramatic format for the purposes of copyright protection to use it to describe the features of a television series which is presented in a particular way with repeated, but unconnected, use of set phrases and with the aid of particular accessories. In essence what the plaintiff sought to do was to isolate certain features of the series from the changing material presented in each show (for example, the performers' acts in each show). The court rejected this approach. The features were too nebulous. The court stated that:

> ... a dramatic work must have sufficient unity to be capable of performance ... the features claimed as constituting the 'format' of a television show being unrelated to each other except as accessories to be used in the presentation of some other dramatic or musical performance, lack the essential characteristic.

Opportunity Knocks was essentially a talent show, the general formula of which is not in itself original. Where the basic idea for an advertisement or promotion is original, or where the new features are more substantial than in the *Opportunity Knocks* case, it is still, it is suggested, possible for a plaintiff to show that copyright subsists in a format. It must, however, be said that any such case would not be an easy one to pursue successfully.

Copyright infringement

Copyright will be infringed where a substantial part of the work has been reproduced without consent. 'Substantial' is a test of the quality of what has been reproduced, rather than the quantity. If a small – but key – part of the material/format is taken, that could infringe copyright in the material.

The fact that copying has taken place must be established. If evidence can be adduced to show that the alleged copyist had access to the material which has been reproduced and that there is sufficient similarity between the copyright work and the alleged copy, that will create an inference that copying has taken place which it will be for the defendant to displace, for example, by showing that its material predates the plaintiff's material.

Hints and tips under copyright law

In order to support a claim under copyright law, material which would help show that the work is original, such as scripts, drafts, briefings, artwork and other relevant documents, should be retained. Details of the identity of the creator(s) and the dates when the work was first put into material form and subsequently amended should also be kept.

The retention of this type of information will also assist those faced with a copyright claim against them in proving that their work has not been copied from the plaintiff's material.

It is advisable that the symbol which denotes the existence of copyright, ©, followed by the copyright owner's name and the year when the work was first created, is used on all works. It should be shown prominently, for example, on any title page or at the foot of artwork. Whilst the symbol does not in itself confer rights on the copyright owner, it informs third parties that copyright is claimed in the material. It can therefore operate as a deterrent.

Further details about copyright infringement claims are contained in Chapter 4.

Breach of confidence

An action for breach of confidence can prevent the unauthorised use of formats even where copyright law does not assist. It will, however, apply only where the idea in question has not been made public.

There is a broad principle recognised in law that a party who receives information in confidence, either directly or indirectly, should not profit from the unauthorised use of that information. The principle applies not only to the original recipient of the information, but also to any subsequent recipient of the information, provided that the subsequent recipients are also on notice of the confidential nature of the information.

The principle requires that the following criteria should be satisfied:

(a) the information must not be known to the general public;

(b) it must have been imparted in circumstances importing an obligation of confidentiality, whether express or implied;

(c) there must be unauthorised use of the information to the detriment of the person who originally supplied it.

The confidential information or idea can be in writing or oral. To be capable of protection, the idea must be sufficiently developed in the sense that it is an identifiable idea which is capable of being realised as an actuality. It should be at a development stage where it has some attractiveness as an advertisement or promotion. This does not necessarily mean that it has to be in the form of a full synopsis or script. It does not necessarily have to be developed to the same extent as would be required under copyright law.

The information must be original in the sense that it is not yet in the public domain. It must also be new. Originality can either mean a significant new twist or slant to a well known concept or a completely new idea.

The obligation of confidence

The obligation of confidence does not have to be expressly provided for. Notwithstanding this, in the interests of certainty it is always preferable to have a written agreement signed by all relevant parties setting out the existence and scope of the duty of confidence.

For the sake of clarity, it will help if confidential material submitted to third parties is clearly labelled as such. An express statement that material is confidential, which is accepted on that basis, will create a presumption that the information has been imparted in confidence.

Case law indicates that where information or ideas of a commercial or industrial value are given on a businesslike basis with some avowed common object in mind, for example, a joint venture, there is a presumption that an obligation of confidence exists even where there is no express obligation set down. Any person seeking to show that there was in fact no implied obligation of confidence, will have a heavy burden to discharge.

In industries where there is generally perceived to be an ethical or moral obligation to treat ideas or information as being submitted in confidence, that perception will give rise to a presumption that an obligation of confidence exists.

How to protect confidential information

The information should be in writing for reasons of certainty. Where disclosures are made orally, they should be confirmed in writing. Confidential information should be clearly labelled as such.

The fact that the information has been submitted in confidence should be stated clearly and in writing. Ideally, a confidentiality agreement should be drawn up and signed by all relevant parties. Such an agreement need not be complex. Where agencies are involved in pitches, they should always require that a confidentiality agreement be signed by the client in respect of all the material which is presented at the pitch.

Confidential information should be kept secure.

Recipients of confidential information

Recipients of information which may be confidential, for example, unsolicited ideas for commercials or promotions, should safeguard their position against claims for breach of confidence which allege that they have made use of ideas submitted to them in confidence.

To help them to rebut the plaintiff's claims, recipients should make a note of exactly what has been disclosed to them, on what basis, by whom by and to whom. Often, claims for breach of confidence are difficult to defend because the defendant has no record of the above details.

All relevant development material should be recorded in writing and retained with a view to demonstrating that the complainant's idea has not been copied or otherwise made use of.

Where recipients do not intend to make use of a proposal which is contained in unsolicited material, the material should be returned to the recipient with a note indicating that the recipient is not interested in the material. The note should state that copies of the material have not been retained. Such a step will help to avoid future proceedings for breach of confidence.

CHAPTER 12

CONTEMPT OF COURT – REFERENCES TO LEGAL PROCEEDINGS IN ADVERTISEMENTS AND PROMOTIONS

In this book, the law relating to contempt of court is considered only in relation to the consequences of publishing material which the law considers might influence the outcome of criminal or civil cases. Other aspects of the law of contempt are unlikely to be relevant to the advertising and promotions industries.

The Contempt of Court Act 1981

This Act sets out the law in relation to contempt of court. Under the Act, a contempt of court is committed if a publication, such as an advertisement, creates a substantial risk that the course of justice in legal proceedings in question will be seriously prejudiced or impeded.

In short, this involves two elements, namely, *substantial risk*, and *serious prejudice*.

Both factors must exist. It is not contempt to publish material which carries a substantial risk of minimal prejudice. Nor is it contempt to publish material with a remote or unlikely risk of serious prejudice.

Under the Act's provisions, liability can attach to statements whether or not there was an intention to prejudice legal proceedings. In addition to the law of contempt, which is set out in the 1981 Act, a non-statute-based type of contempt can be committed where the the maker of the statement had an intention to prejudice legal proceedings.

Serious prejudice

Serious prejudice is of a kind which is likely to influence the actual outcome of the trial, for example, by tipping the verdict of the jury in a criminal or a defamation case.

The criteria for judging serious prejudice will depend on who is sitting in judgment. Juries or lay magistrates are considered to be more susceptible to public comment than judges. A contempt is therefore more likely to be committed in a case which is tried by jury or lay magistrate. For this reason, particular care should be taken when referring to cases which will be tried in that way.

Substantial risk

The risk must be more than remote. The assessment of the degree of risk is made in the particular context of each case and will include such factors as:

(a) The length of time between publication and trial. For example, where there is a delay of many months, the chances of jurors remembering the material will be fairly low.

(b) If the publication is a 'one-off', the chances of it being remembered will be lower than if the alleged contempt is contained in a widely publicised and oft-repeated advertising campaign or promotion.

(c) The size of the circulation of the offending material will be relevant. Generally, the smaller the likely audience, the less likely that the publication will be a contempt.

The type of statement which may be in contempt of court

The following types of statement may be published in contempt of court:

(a) predictions of the outcome of litigation;

(b) attacks on the credibility of witnesses;

(c) unfavourable information about a defendant's history, criminal record, commercial practices or lifestyle;

(d) where the court has placed restrictions on the reporting of any proceedings, the publication of material in contravention of that order will be a contempt.

Proceedings must be active

The Act only applies to contempts which are committed when proceedings are active.

The meaning of active

Proceedings are active where a person has been arrested or charged in *criminal* proceedings or a warrant or summons has been issued. In *civil* (that is, non-criminal) proceedings, an action becomes active where it has been set down for trial. Setting down is a formal step in civil proceedings whereby the parties inform the court that the preliminary stages of the litigation have been completed and that the action is ready for trial. A contempt can be committed *even where it was not intended* once these trigger points have been reached.

In contrast, deliberate contempt of court, that is, where there is an intention to influence proceedings, can be committed at any stage of the proceedings, even before a suspect has been arrested in criminal proceedings.

Defences

The following defences are available:

(a) It is a defence for the advertiser who is charged with contempt under the Act to show that it did not know and had no reason to believe that the case in question was 'active'. This defence will *not* apply unless the advertiser can show that it took all reasonable steps to find out what stage the proceedings had reached.

(b) If the material is a fair and accurate report of the proceedings it will not be contempt, even if its effect is to cause prejudice.

(c) Where material is published as part of a discussion in good faith of public affairs or other matters of general public interest, it will not be a contempt if the risk of prejudice to particular proceedings is incidental to that discussion. This defence is intended to prevent the gagging of *bona fide* discussion on matters of public interest. Where the discussion is focused around a particular case, the defence is unlikely to succeed.

The potential consequences of being in contempt

A publisher in contempt can be made subject to a fine of an unlimited amount. Individuals can also be committed to prison for up to two years. The usual sanction is a large fine. Recent cases against newspapers which have published offending articles have resulted in fines in the region of £40,000–50,000. The court will also usually make an order restraining any repetition of the contempt.

CHAPTER 13

OBSCENITY, INDECENCY AND BLASPHEMY

The laws which apply in relation to obscenity, indecency and blasphemy tend to be directed against sexual explicitness or excessively violent imagery, but they are not confined to those areas. Material that encourages the taking of illegal drugs could in theory be obscene or indecent, as could publications which feature horrific imagery of the kind found in 'horror comics'.

Sanctions for committing offences in relation to the above include imprisonment and/or fines.

OBSCENITY

A publication is obscene if it has a tendency to deprave and corrupt its audience. The publication of obscene material is a *criminal offence* under the Obscene Publications Act 1959. The dominant effect of the publication taken as a whole must be to tend to deprave or corrupt the persons who are likely in all the circumstances to read, see or hear the matter embodied in it. 'Deprave' means to make morally bad or to pervert or debase. 'Corrupt' means to render morally unsound. Both of these concepts go further than merely shocking or disgusting the audience. They require a tendency to lead their audience morally astray. It is the effect of the work which is important. The purpose for which the material was published is irrelevant.

It is a defence to a charge of obscenity to show that the publication of the material was for the public good, for example, in the interests of the arts, science, literature or learning. Any such defence is unlikely to be successful in an advertising or promotions context.

For the purposes of the Act, 'publication' of obscene material extends to the distribution, circulation or sale of the material. It is also an offence to possess obscene material for publication or gain.

INDECENCY

A publication is indecent if it is of a kind that ordinary people would find to offend against recognised standards of propriety (*Knuller v DPP* [1973] AC 435). The publication of indecent material can be a *criminal offence* under the Indecent Displays (Control) Act 1981 as well as under the common law offence of corrupting public morals. It is a criminal offence to send indecent material through the post pursuant to the Post Office Act 1953. As with the law in relation to obscenity, it is the *effect* of the material which is important rather than its intended purpose.

BLASPHEMY

A publication may be blasphemous if it is indecent in a religious context. The publication of blasphemous material will be a *criminal offence*. It is the effect of the material which is important rather than its purpose. Prosecutions for blasphemy are, in practice, extremely rare.

CHAPTER 14

LEGAL PROCEDURE AND REMEDIES

INTRODUCTION

This chapter concerns the remedies available to parties whose rights have been infringed.

It describes the actions that can be taken if your rights have been infringed and what steps might be taken against you if a claim of infringement is made.

The chapter concerns civil remedies only. Sanctions under the various industry Codes are set out below, in Chapters 17–20. The penalties for committing the criminal offences described in the book are set out alongside the description of the offences.

Legal proceedings – what to expect

If a party believes that its rights have been infringed, the most efficacious way of obtaining redress is usually the threat of, or the commencement of, legal proceedings. It is usual to inform the infringing party of the intention to commence proceedings, except where the dispute has to be dealt with urgently or where the opposing party is likely to destroy vital evidence if it is put on notice of the imminent issue of proceedings.

Generally, a *letter before action* (sometimes called a cease and desist letter) will be written to the other party setting out the alleged causes of action against it and requiring written undertakings that it will stop the infringing activities and, where appropriate, that it will pay compensation for any loss that has been suffered as a result of the infringing activities. The form of the letter before action will depend on the nature of the alleged wrong. The letter will usually stipulate a time by which a substantive reply must be received if legal proceedings are to be avoided. Where an allegation of registered trade mark infringement is made, the allegation must be carefully worded. The making of unjustified threats of trade mark infringement is prohibited under the Trade Marks Act 1994 and can be restrained by the court. It is recommended that legal advice is taken before any such allegation is made.

If you receive a letter before action and believe that you are covered by insurance in respect of the claim, you should take immediate steps to inform your insurers of the potential claim. Failure to do so may result in the insurer avoiding the claim.

If a satisfactory response is not received to the letter before action, legal proceedings will generally be commenced.

This chapter describes litigation procedure in the High Court. The procedure is relatively similar in the county court. Some of the causes of action in this book can only be pursued in the High Court, for example, defamation claims.

Proceedings are begun by issuing a *writ of summons*. The writ need only contain a brief indication of the causes of action alleged and the remedies which are sought. Alternatively, it can set out the plaintiff's case in full. The drafting of a writ is a technical matter and, where possible, it should be delegated to a solicitor or a barrister. The party issuing the writ is called the *plaintiff*. The party against whom the writ is issued is the *defendant*. A fee for issuing the writ is payable to the court. The amount is dependent on the amount of compensation sought by the plaintiff, subject to an overall maximum figure of £500 at the date of publication. The amount of the fee will be subject to periodic review.

The writ must be served by the plaintiff on the defendant within four months of the date of issue. The defendant has to acknowledge service of the writ within 14 days of the date when he receives the writ (including the day when it was actually received). Service is acknowledged by completing a prescribed form which accompanies the writ and returning the form to the court. If the form is not returned within the 14 day limit, the plaintiff can enter judgment against the defendant. It is therefore important that the form is completed and sent off to the court in time.

The form for acknowledging service asks the defendant whether it intends to defend the proceedings. If it wishes to do so, the defendant must indicate its intention at the appropriate place on the form. This is known as *giving notice of intention to defend*.

A limited company or a public limited company can lodge the acknowledgment of service on its behalf but thereafter it must be legally represented in the proceedings. Other defendants may represent themselves throughout the proceedings if they choose to do so.

If the writ does not set out the plaintiff's case in full, the plaintiff must serve a separate document known as a *statement of claim*. The statement of claim can be served with the writ or at any time before the expiry of 14 days from the defendant's giving notice of intention to defend.

Upon service of the statement of claim, the defendant has to serve a document setting out its defences to the claim. This document is called a *defence*. It must be served either within 14 days of service of the statement of claim or within 28 days of service of the writ, whichever date is the later. If the defence is not served within this time limit, the plaintiff can enter judgment against the defendant.

The plaintiff can, if appropriate, serve a response to the defence called a *reply*. A reply is not always necessary. Legal advice should be sought about whether service of a reply is appropriate. In defamation cases, where the defendant pleads justification or fair comment, the service of a reply is *obligatory*. The plaintiff to a defamation action must state in the reply which of the facts which the defendant has included in its defence are accepted and which are denied and why they are denied.

Sometimes, the defendant may wish to raise a positive case against the plaintiff. It can do so by serving a *counterclaim*. The counterclaim is generally served with the defence. The counterclaim does not have to have any relationship to the plaintiff's claim. If company A sues B for passing off, B could counterclaim against A for copyright infringement on an unrelated matter. Where a counterclaim is served, the plaintiff must serve a defence to it within 14 days. Failure to do so could result in judgment being entered on the counterclaim.

The statement of claim, defence, reply, counterclaim and defence to counterclaim are known collectively as *pleadings*.

Sometimes, a party will think that the other side's pleading is not sufficiently detailed to allow it to know the case it has to meet. In such circumstances, a *request for further and better particulars* of the pleading can be served. The time limit for answering the request is a matter for agreement between the parties. There is often a technical argument about whether requests for particulars are invalid or unnecessary. Parties to litigation sometimes use the service of requests as a delaying tactic to bog down the proceedings. That is not the appropriate function of the request procedure and the misuse of it in this way can result in cost penalties against the offending party.

Once the defence has been served, the plaintiff should ask the court to lay down a timetable for the future conduct of the action. This application is called the *summons for directions*.

The future conduct of the action will generally involve at least some of the following steps.

Discovery

This is the process where each party to the litigation serves a list of all the documents which are relevant to its case which are in its possession or which it has the right to call for from third parties. The parties cannot pick and choose what goes in the list. The list must include any documents which are unhelpful to a party's case as well as those which are favourable. Once a defendant is put on notice that proceedings may be issued, or as soon as a plaintiff is contemplating litigation, it must not destroy any documents which are, or which may be, relevant to the claim. If it does so, its claim or defence may be struck out.

When lists of documents have been exchanged, each party can inspect the other's documents and take copies of them. Documents obtained on discovery can only be used for the purpose of the litigation for which they have been disclosed unless permission is obtained from the court for their use for another purpose.

Not all of the documents which are relevant have to be made available for inspection. Certain classes of documents are 'privileged' from production. Documents containing legal advice are privileged, as are documents which are brought into existence for the purposes of the legal proceedings.

Service of witness statements

Each party will be required to prepare and serve statements consisting of the evidence which its witnesses will give at trial. The statements must be signed by the witness in question and will usually stand as that witness's evidence-in-chief on which they will be cross-examined. It is therefore important that the statements are accurate and complete.

Service of expert's reports

Where a party wishes to serve expert evidence, for example, about the usual practices in the advertising industry in relation to the matters in dispute, a written report of the evidence must be served on the other parties. The other parties will usually want to serve expert evidence in response. In complex cases, it is often helpful for the experts for all of the parties to meet, to narrow down the issues in dispute between them. Sometimes, the court will insist that such a meeting take place. Leave is required from the court before expert evidence can be adduced.

Setting down

Setting down is the process whereby the court is formally notified that the case is ready for trial. Upon being set down, the case enters the list of cases waiting for a trial date to be allotted to them.

Third party proceedings

The defendant may wish to join a third party into the proceedings where that party bears some responsibility for the alleged wrong. For example, if company X is sued for copyright infringement in respect of its advertisements, it may join its advertising agency as third parties to the dispute. It will do this by way of service of a *third party notice*. The third party is effectively a defendant to the proceedings and the procedural steps set out above will apply to it in the same way as to the principal parties.

Time limits

The time limits set out above are not set in stone. Parties can agree extensions of time or applications can be made to the court for extensions in appropriate circumstances.

Summary judgment

Where the plaintiff can demonstrate that the defendant has no arguable defence to its claim, it can obtain summary judgment against the defendant at any time after the defendant has given notice of intention to defend the proceedings. The procedure is not presently available for defamation claims. The application can be made before the defendant has served its defence. The evidence in support of, and against, the application is generally in the form of sworn written statements of evidence known as *affidavits*.

The Defamation Act 1996 makes provision for the introduction of a summary judgment procedure for defamation claims, although it is not yet in place. At present it is expected that there will be a £10,000 limit for damages awards for defamation cases under the summary procedure. To obtain summary judgment in a defamation claim the plaintiff will have to show that the defence has no reasonable prospect of success.

Costs of litigation

The general rule is that the unsuccessful party to litigation pays the costs of the successful party, although this rule is always subject to the court's discretion. The costs which the losing party will have to pay will not be the total amount of the successful party's costs. The court assesses the amount of costs which the losing party must pay in a process known as *taxation*. As a rule of thumb, the winning party can expect to obtain an order that it can recover about two-thirds of its costs from the unsuccessful party, leaving a shortfall of one-third which it will have to pay itself.

Where the unsuccessful party is in receipt of legal aid, it is unlikely that any of the successful party's costs will be recoverable. The successful party will usually have to pay all its costs.

Payment into court

A payment into court is an important tactic available to a defendant. It involves the defendant assessing the value of the plaintiff's claim. The defendant then pays that sum into court and serves a notice informing the plaintiff that it has done so. The plaintiff has 21 days to accept the sum. If it does not do so, and is awarded at trial a sum in compensation which is equal to or the same as the amount of the payment in, the plaintiff will generally be ordered to pay the defendant's costs from the date of the payment in.

Where the claim against the defendant involves elements other than a claim for money, for example, a claim for an injunction or for delivery up (see below), the notice of payment in should be accompanied by a letter offering undertakings which address those claims. Such a letter is known as a *Calderbank* letter.

A payment into court is not an admission of liability. The court will not know about the payment until it has reached a judgment in favour of the plaintiff. If the defendant is successful in its defence, the court will never know about the payment in.

Appeals

The Court of Appeal hears appeals from the High Court. Permission (or leave) is required before an appeal can be made. The trial judge can grant leave, although in practice he rarely does so. The more usual procedure is to make an application to the Court of Appeal for leave to appeal to it. If the application for leave is successful the appeal can go ahead. Appeals from the Court of Appeal can be made to the House of Lords. Leave will be required from the House of Lords. Leave to appeal will generally only be granted by the House of Lords in respect of cases which raise issues of public importance which go beyond the particular dispute in question.

Monetary compensation

The plaintiff will invariably claim compensation for loss suffered as a result of the defendant's wrongdoing. This can take the form of a claim for damages or, in some cases, an account of profit.

Damages

Damages are awarded to compensate the successful party. They are not intended to punish the defendant (except in the case of an award of exemplary damages: see below, p 146). Generally, the measure is the sum required to put the plaintiff in the position it would have been in if the defendant had not infringed its rights. In a case of copyright or trade mark infringement the starting point will be the licence fee which would have been agreed between the parties if the plaintiff had licensed the defendant's infringing use.

Defamation claims

In claims for defamation, a jury usually assesses damages. They are intended to compensate the plaintiff for damage to reputation. Very high awards of damages have attracted a good deal of press attention in recent years. That trend seems to be disappearing, at least in cases where damages awards are appealed. The Court of Appeal has the power to alter the amount of damages in libel cases and has done so in a number of recent high profile cases, for example, on an appeal by Mirror Group Newspapers against an award of damages to Esther Rantzen the damages award at trial was reduced from £250,000 to £110,000 (Rantzen v Mirror Group Newspapers [1993] 4 All ER 375). Similarly, an award to Elton John was reduced from £75,000 to £25,000 (Elton John v MGN Ltd [1996] 3 WLR 593). In practice, many cases which attract publicity for high awards of damages are settled for very much reduced sums pending an appeal hearing.

An additional reason for the trend in the reduction of damages awards in defamation cases is that the jury can now be directed by the judge as to a suitable bracket for an award for compensation (although the final decision still rests with the jury, which does not have to follow the judge's direction). In particular, the jury can be directed to compare the level of damages likely to be awarded in personal injury cases with damage to the plaintiff's reputation. The top of the range for such awards in respect of physical injuries such as quadriplegia or total blindness and deafness is £130,000. Whilst this figure is not intended to be a ceiling on libel awards, it will, it is hoped, assist juries in keeping awards of damages in defamation cases in proportion to other types of awards.

Account of profit

When claims are made for copyright infringement, passing off, trade mark infringement or breach of confidence the plaintiff can ask for an account of profit as an alternative to damages. The account will require the defendant to account to the plaintiff for the profit which it has made as a result of its infringing activities.

The plaintiff will not normally have to elect damages or an account until after liability has been determined. It is important that a plaintiff makes it clear in its initial writ that it may seek damages or at its election an account of profit in order to keep its options open.

Additional damages

Additional damages are only available in claims for copyright infringement where the infringement is particularly serious (or flagrant), for example, cases of intentional infringement. Additional damages must be specifically claimed in the writ. They are not available where the plaintiff elects for an account of profit.

Exemplary damages

Exemplary damages are awarded to the plaintiff in order to punish the defendant. They can only be awarded in a limited number of defined situations. The most relevant situation is where the defendant can be proved to have taken a cynical decision to infringe the plaintiff's rights in the belief that the amount of damages it will have to pay will be exceeded by the amount of profit that will accrue to the defendant; for example, where the defendant takes a decision to publish a defamatory statement knowing that the profits that will accrue from it doing so will be greater than the damages which will be awarded against it. Exemplary damages have to be specifically claimed in the writ.

Injunctions

An injunction is an order of the court. It can take a number of forms. It can be prohibitory, which means that it will restrain the defendant from carrying out the act complained of, or mandatory, which means that it will require the defendant to take a positive step, usually to rectify its wrongdoing.

Injunctions can be awarded at the conclusion of legal proceedings when liability has been determined. Such injunctions are called *final injunctions*. A plaintiff who is successful at trial will not be entitled to an injunction as of right. The court will only grant an injunction where it is in the interests of justice to do so.

Legal proceedings can often take over a year to come to trial. Often, a plaintiff will wish to take steps to restrain the defendant's activities before trial, for example, to prevent the defendant from launching its new advertising campaign which the plaintiff alleges is an infringement of its copyright. If the plaintiff had to wait until the trial of the action for its injunction, the offending campaign is likely to have been both launched and completed before the plaintiff can claim its injunction. In such cases the court can award *interlocutory injunctions* which will take effect until the trial of the action.

Interlocutory injunctions can be obtained very quickly and in cases of sufficient urgency without notice to the other side.

Where injunctions are obtained without notice to the other side, or without giving the other side sufficient time to prepare its opposition to the application, the injunction will only remain in place until the other side has an opportunity to resist the application at a hearing where both parties are represented. The court can decide at such a hearing to continue the interlocutory injunction until trial or to lift it.

If the plaintiff is successful in obtaining an interlocutory injunction, it will be required to give an undertaking to the court that it will compensate the defendant for the loss that it suffers as a result of the interlocutory injunction being in place if a final injunction is not awarded at trial. The plaintiff must be able to satisfy the court that it has the means to satisfy the cross undertaking.

When considering whether to grant an interlocutory injunction, the court will consider the following matters:

(a) Does the plaintiff have a real prospect of obtaining an injunction at trial in the sense that it is able to demonstrate that it has an arguable case? Where the interlocutory injunction will in practice be the final determination of the dispute and the case is unlikely to proceed further if the injunction is granted, the court will probably assess the relative merits of the parties' cases and require that the plaintiff shows more than just an arguable case.

(b) If an interlocutory injunction is not awarded, will the plaintiff be adequately compensated by an award of damages at trial, or will it suffer unquantifiable or irreparable harm which cannot be compensated by damages? If the plaintiff will be adequately compensated by damages, no interlocutory injunction should be awarded.

(c) If the plaintiff would not be adequately compensated by damages, the court must ask whether the defendant would be adequately compensated by the plaintiff's cross-undertaking in damages for the loss it suffers whilst the interlocutory injunction is in force if a final injunction is not made against it at trial. If the answer is yes, an interlocutory injunction should be awarded.

(d) If damages will not fully compensate either party, the court may consider other factors, such as the maintenance of the status quo.

(e) Where the injunction is in practice likely to be the end of the proceedings, the successful party should consider seeking an order that its costs be paid by the losing party at the conclusion of the injunction hearing.

Breach of an injunction

The breach of an injunction is a contempt of court and potentially punishable by imprisonment or by an unlimited fine.

Delivery up

Delivery up is the sanction whereby the defendant is ordered to deliver up and forfeit all infringing material or to destroy the infringing material on oath. As with an injunction, the breach of such an order is a contempt of court.

Mediation and alternative dispute resolution

In appropriate cases, parties to a dispute should consider whether there is any scope for resolution through an alternative to litigation, for example, through the use of mediation procedures. As part of the litigation process, the parties are required at least to consider the option, if only to discount it.

CHAPTER 15

JUDICIAL REVIEW

REVIEWING DECISIONS UNDER THE INDUSTRY CODES OF PRACTICE

The Advertising Standards Authority, the Independent Television Commission and the Radio Authority are all subject to judicial review by the High Court. The court has not yet had to consider whether ICSTIS are also subject to judicial review but, by analogy, it is likely to be so. In practice, judicial review is the only mechanism for disgruntled advertisers who wish to apply to the courts for redress against adverse decisions under the industry Codes of Practice. Judicial review is *not* a right of appeal against adverse findings by the regulatory bodies. It will only arise in certain limited circumstances and, even if the application is successful, it will not result in the court substituting its decision in place of the authorities' decision. An application for judicial review is not permitted without leave of the court. There are two main circumstances where an application for judicial review might be appropriate.

The authority has not acted fairly

The application for judicial review may be made on the ground that the authority in question has not acted fairly when reaching its decision. The applicant might claim that it was denied a fair hearing, for example, because it was not fully informed of the case that it had to meet, or that it was not given a proper opportunity to correct or contradict that case.

A right to an oral hearing?

None of the authorities allows a right to an oral hearing under the provisions of their Codes. An advertiser which has requested an oral hearing from the relevant authority will not necessarily be able to claim that it has not been given a fair hearing if its request is denied. In general, the courts will accept that a decision based on written representations will be fair where an oral hearing would not be practical. In order to show that the authority has acted unfairly, the applicant for judicial review must be able to show that there were special circumstances why a hearing on paper was inadequate in their particular case and that these circumstances were brought to the attention of the authority. The court must then determine whether the authority acted unfairly when it denied an oral hearing to the advertiser.

The authority has not exercised its discretion in a reasonable manner

This is the second ground in respect of which an application for judicial review might lie. Each of the authorities in question is under a duty to act reasonably when reaching their decisions. Where the authority reaches a decision which no reasonable authority would have come to, for example, because it did not consider certain pieces of evidence, or it placed too much weight on one relevant factor, or it acted on irrelevant grounds, an application can be made to the courts that the decision be quashed.

Effects of judicial review

Where a successful application is made for judicial review, the court will quash the original decision of the authority. It will not substitute its decision in its place. Instead, the decision may be remitted back to the authority to reconsider in the light of the court's findings. The decision of the authority may be the same at the end of the day. The effect of the judicial review application may only be to change the way in which the decision is reached.

Interlocutory injunctions and judicial review

It is possible for advertisers to obtain interlocutory injunctions to restrain the publication of an adverse decision in the authority's reports whilst an application for judicial review is pending. Direct Line Financial Services Limited recently applied for judicial review in respect of a decision of the ASA. It also obtained an injunction against the ASA which resulted in the pulping of the relevant monthly report and its republication in an amended form without reference to the Direct Line Financial Services decision, pending the judicial review hearing. Advertisers who are tempted to try a similar tactic should bear in mind that they will be asked to give an undertaking to compensate the authority for its losses if the application for judicial review turns out to be unsuccessful. The losses in question may be considerable.

CHAPTER 16

EUROPEAN LAW –
HARMONY THROUGHOUT EUROPE?

PAN-EUROPEAN ADVERTISING CAMPAIGNS

This chapter examines the extent to which a uniform body of advertising and sales promotion law exists in Europe. Cross-border promotional activities are becoming increasingly common throughout the European Union. But to what extent are differing national restrictions creating obstacles to such activities? This issue is also becoming increasingly relevant because of the growth of the internet as a sales promotion medium.

The chapter also examines legislative developments in the European Commission which are likely to be incorporated into UK national law in the relatively near future and looks at the likely effects of the developments for UK national law.

The European Community ideal – free movement of goods and services

The free movement of goods and services is a fundamental principle of the European Community (now the European Union). It is enshrined in the EC Treaty (the document which established the European Community). The national advertising, sales promotion and marketing laws of the countries which make up the European Community are subject to the free movement principle. Restrictions that operate to prevent the free movement of advertising or marketing campaigns throughout the Community are in breach of the free movement principle unless there is an overriding public interest which justifies their existence. Even then, restrictions must apply equally to the domestic goods/services of the country in question as to goods/services imported from other Member States and must be proportionate to the objectives which they are intended to achieve.

In practice, there is a wide discrepancy between the national laws of EC Member States. In many cases the discrepancies make pan-European advertising impossible. The many differences between national laws of the various States are set out in a document, produced by the Institute of Sales Promotion, entitled 'the European Promotional Legislation Guide'. Many of the differences which exist cannot be justified under the free movement of goods principles.

Successful challenges to national advertising laws under the EC Treaty have been made to the European Court of Justice (ECJ). Litigation through the ECJ is a complex, expensive and lengthy process. The body of law that has emerged from the ECJ over the years is by no means consistent. There will therefore be an element of uncertainty for advertisers who choose to challenge national laws of Member States by this route.

STEPS TOWARDS HARMONISATION

For some years now, the Commission (which is the body within the Community which initiates and implements legislation) has embarked on a programme of legislative change in relation to marketing and intellectual property considerations which are intended to harmonise the national laws of Member States. The harmonisation programme is being carried out piecemeal and is still not complete. It has already made certain important changes which operate to facilitate cross-border marketing activity. Other important changes are in the pipeline for the future. The relevant measures are likely to be, or have been, implemented by way of *directives*. Directives are not automatically enforceable by EC Member States, although they are binding on the States to which they are addressed. Member States are obliged to implement directives by way of their own national legislation. The Commission will usually stipulate a time by which the directive has to have been implemented by each Member State. Parties who suffer loss as a result of the late implementation of, or the failure to implement, a directive by a Member State may be able to recover against that State for its loss.

Directives are published in the *Official Journal of the Community*.

Important directives are as follows.

Misleading advertising

Council Directive of 10 September 1984 relating to the approximation of the laws of Member States concerning misleading advertising (84/450/EEC OJ L250) was intended to establish a minimum standard for the laws, regulations and administrative provisions concerning misleading advertising throughout the Community. It was seen as a first step towards harmonisation. The preamble to the Directive envisages a second step as being a separate directive to harmonise the laws on unfair advertising and comparative advertising (of which more later).

The Directive was implemented in the UK by the Control of Misleading Advertisements Regulations 1988 SI 1988/915, which are discussed in Chapter 7.

The harmonising effect of the Directive has in practice been minimal. The Directive did not preclude Member States from retaining or adopting measures which will give more extensive protection to consumers. In practice, the Directive lays down a minimum standard for each State. The laws of some States may go much further.

Advertisers should therefore check the national laws of each relevant State in relation to the regulation of misleading advertisements to ensure that their advertising complies with them.

Comparative advertising

A directive has been adopted[1] which makes amendments to the Misleading Advertising Directive considered above. The amendments are intended to harmonise the laws relating to comparative advertising throughout Member States. The amendments have been in draft form for a long time, having first been proposed as long ago as 1984. They were finalised in October 1997 and are due to be implemented by Member States by the year 2000.

The provisions of the Directive, and their likely effect on UK law, are discussed in Chapter 8. Whilst the provisions may increase the restrictions on comparative advertising in some countries (including, possibly, the UK), they are to be welcomed by advertisers who wish to use cross-border comparative advertising because of the consistency in approach which they are intended to achieve.

Unfair advertising

A draft directive designed to implement harmonised laws to regulate unfair advertising has been dropped by the commission because of a failure of the Member States to reach agreement on its content. So far as the writer is aware, there are no firm plans to revive such a directive which, if implemented, would have been likely to have made changes to UK law which would have significantly restricted the freedom of advertisers.

Distance selling

There is a draft directive in existence which is intended to harmonise the laws relating to distance selling throughout Member States. Its terms are not yet finalised at the time of writing. In particular, the author understands that there is a dispute between Member States about whether the Directive will apply to financial services. The Distance Selling Directive is intended to apply

---

[1]   Directive 97/55, amending Directive 84/450.

to consumer contracts which are negotiated at a distance. It will, when implemented, catch most forms of direct marketing, for example, telesales, catalogue marketing, marketing over the internet, offers contained in newspapers, flyers, etc.

It will apply to national and pan-European direct marketing. The UK Government will be obliged to implement or amend legislation to bring the terms of the Directive into force. Although the provisions of the Directive have not been finalised, the bulk of them are unlikely to change significantly. The principal provisions are as follows:

(a) All communications at a distance must make their commercial purpose clear.

(b) Cold calling through telephone, fax or e-mail must not be used unless the consumer has consented.

(c) The consumer must be told the following information:

- the identity of the supplier (with full name and address);
- the main characteristics of the product or service;
- the price, quantity and any transport charges;
- the payment and delivery arrangements;
- the cooling off provision (see (e) below);
- the period for which solicitation remains valid.

(d) Suppliers cannot insist on prepayments.

(e) Consumers must have a cooling off period of at least seven days.

(f) Where unsolicited goods are delivered, consumers may do what they wish with them unless there has been an obvious mistake.

(g) Performance of the contract must begin within 30 days after the order has been received, unless clearly indicated otherwise.

(h) All contractual information (including details of guarantees) must be supplied in writing no later than the time of delivery.

A change in emphasis – the Green Paper on Commercial Communications COM (96) 192

In 1992, the Commission embarked on a review of its policy in the field of commercial communications (to include advertising and marketing). The results of its review were published in the Commission Green Paper entitled *Commercial Communications in the Internal Market in 1996*. This was a discussion document circulated widely amongst the relevant industries for comments. It is expected that formal public hearings will be held in respect of the proposals, which were set out in the Paper during 1998. The Paper made two key proposals as follows:

(a) There should be a uniform assessment methodology established to analyse restrictions which exist under national laws to the free circulation of commercial communications, with a view to determining whether the restrictions are compatible with the EC Treaty.

(b) Restrictions can be challenged if they are incompatible with the EC Treaty provided that they cannot be justified by overriding public interest grounds and/or are disproportionate to their objectives, the intention being that offending restrictions will be dismantled.

What does this mean in practice?

In short, the Commission has proposed the abolition of all restrictions to commercial communications which cannot be justified. This is a more broad brush approach than piecemeal amendment to existing national law. The criteria for the justification are qualitative. In assessing the issue of proportionality, one would look at the objective of the measure and ask whether the measure is in fact linked to the objective, whether it affects other relevant objectives and whether the measure is efficient in meeting its pursued objective. It would also examine whether the restriction will cause a potential chain reaction in other areas of the market.

Example

Country A operates regulations which limit the advertising of alcohol. The objectives of the measure are to deter adults from excessive drinking of alcoholic drinks and to deter children from drinking at all. The methodology proposed in the Green Paper would involve an assessment of whether the restriction on alcohol advertising is linked to its objective. In making this assessment, regard should be had to any research which was undertaken prior to the restriction coming into force, any contemporaneous explanations or justifications for it, the context in which it came into being, etc. If the measure is not linked to its objectives, it runs the risk of being found to be arbitrary and therefore disproportionate. The methodology would also involve an examination of whether the restriction affected other objectives, which would involve a balancing exercise between competing interests, such as the interests of alcohol manufacturers and retailers, vis à vis the health and social considerations behind the measures. The efficiency of the restriction in meeting its objectives would also be assessed. Inefficient restrictions are likely to be struck down.

Whilst the tone of the Green Paper is unnecessarily complex and technical, the basic approach is innovative and laudable. It remains to be seen whether it is taken further and, if so, whether it will be workable in practice.

Television advertising

The Television Without Frontiers Directive was adopted in 1992 (89/552/EEC). It has been implemented in most Member States, including the UK. Its aim is to ensure the free movement of TV broadcasts throughout the Community so that a broadcaster licensed to transmit in one Member State is free to transmit programmes throughout the Community. Amendments to the Directive were agreed in April 1997. They are meant to be implemented by the end of 1998.

The fundamental principle of the Directive is that responsibility for the content of transmissions (to include advertisements) which are carried on a television channel rests with the country of origin of the broadcast rather than the country of reception. If advertising copy is cleared in the State where the advertisement originates, the broadcaster is free to broadcast the advertisement throughout the EU.

When the Directive was going through the review process which led up to its recent amendment, the principle of country of origin came under attack. There was a move towards allowing receiving countries to impose their own restrictions on advertisements. Happily for those advertisers who advertise on pan-European channels, the principle of country of origin has been preserved.

INTELLECTUAL PROPERTY HARMONISATION

Trade marks

Readers are referred to Chapter 1 for details of the Trade Marks Act 1994. That Act is the UK measure which implements the Directive to harmonise the laws of the Member States relating to trade marks (Directive 89/104). The Directive has theoretically brought the law relating to trade marks into line throughout the Union. In practice, it may not have done. Advertisers should check to see whether the national States concerned have implemented the Directive into their national law. Even if it has been implemented, Member States may not interpret the provisions in a uniform manner.

The difference in interpretation is most significant in relation to the meaning of 'association'. The Directive provides that it is an infringement to use a mark which is identical to a registered trade mark in respect of goods or services which are similar to those for which it is registered, or to use a mark which is similar to the registered trade mark in respect of goods or services which are identical or similar to the registered trade mark, where there exists a likelihood of confusion on the part of the public which includes the likelihood of association.

National opinions differ as to what is meant by 'association'. It is widely believed that the concept originates from the law of the Benelux States, which provides that association can exist without the necessity for confusion. Under Benelux law, where a mark brings into mind a registered trade mark without actually generating any confusion it will be an infringement of the trade mark. This substantially extends the rights of the owner of a registered trade mark. The Benelux interpretation of the meaning of 'association' was rejected so far as English national law is concerned by the English courts in the *Wagamama* case (see Chapter 1 for details). In the *Wagamama* case, the court held that there is no infringement of a registered trade mark under English law unless the mark confuses the public into thinking that the goods/services in relation to which a mark is used are connected with the registered trade mark owner.

The approach taken by the English court will not be consistent with the way that the Directive is applied in other Member States. In particular, the Benelux States continue to apply their interpretation of 'association'. Some Member States will therefore give wider protection to registered trade mark owners than others. In order to have a uniform interpretation of the Directive across the EU, the ECJ will have to give a definitive ruling on its meaning which would then be binding on all countries. No such opportunity has arisen for it to do so at the time of writing.

Advertising parallel imported products

A registered trade mark is not infringed under EC law when it is used in relation to goods which were originally put on the market anywhere in the EU under the trade mark by the trade mark owner or with the trade mark owner's consent. Such goods are known as parallel imports.

In the case of *Parfum Christian Dior SA v Evora BV* C-337/95, the ECJ held that, where trade marked goods had been put on the market in a Member State with the trade mark owner's consent, a re-seller, being free to re-sell the goods in the European Union, was also free to make use of the trade mark in advertising material. The case concerned an action by Christian Dior against a business called Evora, which operates a chain of chemist's shops in the Netherlands. Evora obtained Dior products by means of parallel imports. They sold the products in their chemist's shops by reference to advertising material which Evora prepared using pictures of the Dior products. The products which were shown in the advertising featured certain of Dior's trade marks which were registered in the Netherlands. Dior claimed that the advertising material was of inferior quality and was not in keeping with the products' image as luxurious and superior products. It commenced proceedings, alleging that the advertising material was an infringement of its trade mark registrations. The ECJ found that there was no infringement. Evora were entitled to use the trade marks in advertising material. The court recognised that there could be cases where specific circumstances could be proved to show that use of the trade mark would seriously damage the reputation of the trade mark. In such cases, the use of the mark *might* amount to infringement. On the facts of the *Dior* case, Dior had not proved that the reputation of their trade mark had been seriously damaged.

The Community Trade Mark

Trade marks are national rights. This means, for example, that a registration on the French trade mark register will not give the trade mark owner the right to enforce its trade mark in other countries. However, there is now a new Community Trade Mark system for the EU which for the first time makes it possible to obtain a single registration having effect throughout the whole of the EU. The Community Trade Mark system runs in parallel to national trade mark systems. It is not a substitute for them.

The Community Trade Mark system has been slow to get off the ground. The Community Trade Mark office, which is based in Alicante in Spain, has been inundated with applications, which has resulted in a huge backlog. It is too early to judge how the system will work in practice.

Advertisers must now take care to check not only national trade mark registers for the countries in which they wish to advertise to ensure that their advertisements do not infringe a registered trade mark, but also to check the Community Trade Mark register. This can be done at the UK Trade Mark Registry or through most trade mark agents. A Community Trade Mark may be infringed if it is used anywhere in the Community. The definition of infringement is the same as under UK law (the reader is referred to Chapter 1 for further details). If advertisers wish to make use of a mark which is identical or similar to a Community Trade Mark it is recommended that legal advice be sought before they do so.

Copyright

The Commission has done much to harmonise copyright law throughout the EU by adopting the following pieces of community legislation: Council Resolution of 14 May 1992 on increased protection for copyright and neighbouring rights OJ C138/1, 1992, Council Directive of 19 November 1992 on rental right and lending right and on certain rights related to copyright in the field of intellectual property OJ L346/100, 1992 and Council Directive of 11 March 1996 on the legal protection of databases OJ L77/20, 1996. Directives have been adopted to bring the term of protection for copyright into line and to harmonise the existence of certain classes of performers' rights and moral rights. A uniform right of copyright has been established in respect of databases and the ownership of copyright in films has been brought into line. Not all national States have fully implemented all the relevant Directives at the time of writing, although they are obliged to do so. The Directives have been implemented into UK law and the reader is referred to Chapter 4 for an explanation of the effects of their provisions.

As with trade mark law, the extent to which harmonisation is achieved in practice will depend on the different interpretations which are given by national courts to the national laws which implement the Directives, subject to definitive guidance by the ECJ.

PART TWO

THE INDUSTRY CODES

This book is concerned with four sets of Codes. These are:

(a) the British Codes of Advertising and Sales Promotion operated by the Committee of Advertising Practice (CAP);

(b) the Independent Television Commission (ITC) Codes of Advertising Standards and Practice and Programme Sponsorship;

(c) the Radio Authority Advertising and Sponsorship Code; and

(d) the Independent Committee for the Supervision of Standards of Telephone Information Services (ICSTIS) Code of Practice.

Whilst none of these Codes has the force of law, their importance must not be overlooked. A failure to comply with the relevant Codes often results in the withdrawal of advertisements as well as adverse publicity for the advertiser and its agency.

It is important to appreciate that the legal issues, which were considered in the first part of this book, run parallel with the Codes. Compliance with the Codes will not automatically provide a defence to a legal action. Non-compliance will not necessarily mean that a legal wrong has been committed.

CHAPTER 17

THE BRITISH CODES OF ADVERTISING AND SALES PROMOTION

The British Codes of Advertising and Sales Promotion (the Codes) are drawn up and administered by the Committee of Advertising Practice (CAP). The Advertising Standards Authority (ASA) considers complaints which are made under the Codes. A full set of the Codes, and of ASA adjudications, are available free of charge from the ASA's website (www.asa.org.uk) or by telephoning the CAP/ASA Secretariat on 0171 580 5555.

The CAP is made up of representatives from the advertising, direct marketing, sales promotion and media industries. The Codes are therefore drawn up by members of the industries to which they apply.

The Codes are due to be revised in 1999.

Copy advice service

The CAP offers a free copy advice service to advertisers and agencies to help them comply with the Codes. The taking of advice is not mandatory, except in relation to tobacco products, where the CAP must pre-clear advertisements. If copy advice is taken about advertisements for non-tobacco products, it does not have to be followed. The fact that advice has been taken from the CAP will not prevent complaints being upheld by the ASA. Help notes on relevant topics are produced by CAP and are available free of charge by contacting CAP on 0171 580 4100.

The ASA

The ASA is independent of the CAP. It is charged with ensuring that the Codes work in the public interest. It is most associated with its role in considering, and adjudicating on, complaints made under the Codes. The ASA is the final arbiter on the interpretation of the Codes.

Complaints under the Codes

The ASA Council considers complaints made under the Codes. It can also consider advertisements or promotions on its own initiative.

Complaints can be made by any entity. They are often made by trade competitors. It is often cheaper and quicker for a competitor to complain about an advertisement through the ASA rather than to litigate through the courts. There is a requirement that industry complainants should, wherever possible, endeavour to resolve their differences between themselves or through any relevant trade or professional organisations before complaining to the ASA. Trading standards departments or other interested organisations often make complaints to the ASA. Many complaints are made by members of the public and the ASA promote the complaints system to members of the public to encourage them to make use of it.

Sanctions for breach of the Codes

The following sanctions apply to advertisers who are in breach of the Codes:

(a) Advertisers are requested by the ASA to withdraw any advertisement or promotion which breaches the Codes or to amend it to ensure that it does comply. Copy advice is available from the CAP to advise advertisers how to make adequate amendments.

(b) An adverse finding by the ASA will generate publicity. Adjudications are published monthly. The monthly reports give details of the advertisers or promoters and their agencies. The reports are widely available and are circulated as a matter of course to the media, the advertising industry, consumer bodies and government agencies. Adverse adjudications often receive extensive media coverage. Details of ASA adjudications are also published on the ASA's web site.

(c) If advertisers refuse to amend or withdraw offending advertisements, there are a number of measures which can be taken against them including:

- *The enforcement of contractual requirements for compliance with the Codes.* The ASA will ask the CAP to inform its members about the advertiser's non-compliance with its decision. Most media organisations have a term in their standard conditions of business that advertisers or promoters must comply with the Codes. If advertisements have been found not to comply, advertisers may find that they are in breach of this provision and that their advertisements are denied advertising space. The Royal Mail may also withdraw mailsort contracts where advertisers or promoters are in breach.

- *Removal of trade incentives.* For example, membership of trade or professional associations may be jeopardised.

- *Legal proceedings.* The ASA can refer a *misleading* advertisement (but not a promotion) to the Office of Fair Trading (OFT) under the Control of Misleading Advertisement Regulations 1988. It regularly does so in relation to persistent or deliberate offenders. At the time of writing, the ASA had referred approximately nine such advertisers to the OFT. The OFT can obtain an injunction under the regulations to prevent the advertiser using the offending advertisement in the future. The Control of Misleading Advertisements Regulations are considered in detail in Chapter 7.

- Advertisers who produce offensive or irresponsible posters can be subject to compulsory pre-vetting for up to two years by the CAP copy advice team (as from 1 June 1998).

There is no provision for a direct financial penalty for non-compliance with the Codes although the sanctions may cause an indirect financial loss.

The application of the Codes

The Codes apply to advertisements and promotions appearing in the following media in the UK:

(a) newspapers, periodicals and magazines, including specialist and trade publications (subject to certain exceptions relating to the advertisement of medicines to the medical professions);

(b) inserts in printed publications;

(c) posters;

(d) cinema;

(e) video;

(f) non-broadcast electronic media to include video games and the internet;

(g) mailshots;

(h) direct marketing;

(i) brochures, leaflets and circulars;

(j) aerial announcements;

(k) catalogues, including individual entries in catalogues;

(l) viewdata services;

(m) all other types of printed publications including printed directories;

(n) literature sent out as a follow-up to an advertisement.

The Codes *do not* apply to the following:

(a) commercials on television or the radio;

(b) the contents of premium rate telephone services;

(c) advertisements in foreign media;

(d) private classified advertisements – this does not include advertisements placed by commercial dating agencies which are covered by the Codes;

(e) flyposting;

(f) press releases and public relations material;

(g) packaging, *unless* it advertises a sales promotion or is visible as an advertisement;

(h) point of sale displays, *unless* it is otherwise covered by the Sales Promotion Code or the Cigarette Code (see below);

(i) oral communications, for example, telemarketing;

(j) private correspondence;

(k) official notices;

(l) health-related claims in advertisements and promotions addressed only to the medical or allied professions;

(m) the editorial content of books and newspapers.

What is an advertisement for the purposes of the Codes?

Although 'advertisement' is a fundamental concept, it is not defined in the Codes. ASA decisions suggest that statements which would not be termed 'advertisements' in common parlance may be governed by the Codes.

Examples

The complaint concerned a banner on the front cover of the *Radio Times* which made the following claim: 'THE BEST ALL-CHANNEL MAGAZINE'. The complainant challenged the claim on the basis that the magazine did not contain listings for every satellite and cable channel. The complaint was upheld.

The advertisers argued that the ASA had no jurisdiction to consider the complaint at all because the statement in question was not an advertisement for the magazine. The ASA disagreed. It stated that the front page banner fell within the scope of the Codes because it would be seen as an advertisement for the magazine (*BBC Worldwide Publishing t/a Radio Times – ASA Monthly Report No 75, August 1997*).

Similarly, in the *Essex Chronicle* decision, the ASA considered a complaint about a front page banner which described the *Essex Chronicle* as BRITAIN'S TOP-SELLING WEEKLY NEWSPAPER. The complaint was upheld. The ASA did not decline jurisdiction on the ground that the banner was not an advertisement (*Essex Chronicle Series Ltd t/a Essex Chronicle – ASA Monthly Report No 74, July 1997*).

The implication of these decisions is that statements on product packaging are capable of being advertisements which must comply with the provisions of the Codes.

What is a sales promotion?

Sales promotions are defined as promotional marketing techniques which generally involve the provision of a range of direct or indirect additional benefits, usually on a temporary basis, which are designed to make goods or services more attractive to purchasers.

Promotions that are governed by the Codes include reduced price offers, free offers, samples, coupons, promotions with prizes and 'two for the price of one' offers. Also included are incentive schemes, for example, supermarket bonus or loyalty schemes and trade incentive schemes.

General points about the interpretation of the Codes

(a) Conformity with the Codes is assessed by looking at the advertisement or promotion as a whole.

(b) Conformity is assessed by looking at advertisements and promotions in the context in which they appear.

(c) The Codes are designed to be interpreted flexibly. It follows that the *spirit* of the Codes must be complied with as well as the letter.

(d) The intention of the advertiser is irrelevant. Breaches can be committed accidentally.

The Codes' basic principles

The Codes set out a number of basic principles as follows:

(a) advertisements/promotions must be legal, decent, honest and truthful;

(b) they must be prepared with a sense of responsibility to consumers and to society;

(c) they should respect the principles of fair competition generally accepted in business;

(d) they should not bring advertising or sales promotion into disrepute;

(e) they must conform to the Codes.

THE ADVERTISING CODE – A DETAILED EXAMINATION

Preliminary points

Primary responsibility for ensuring compliance with the Advertising Code rests with the advertiser. A close watching brief should therefore be kept on agencies which the advertiser engages for its advertising work. Responsibility for compliance with the Code cannot be abrogated by the engagement of outside professionals.

Advertisers must be able to demonstrate to the ASA that they have complied with the Code. If the ASA requires evidence of compliance, it should be furnished without delay.

Set out below is an analysis of the detailed rules. The rules should not be considered in isolation of each other. The Code as a whole is indivisible.

The rules relating to the use of people in advertisements and the making of comparisons in advertisements are set out in Chapters 10 and 8 respectively.

Legality

The Code states that advertisements must contain nothing that breaks the law or incites others to break it.

Advertisers must comply with all relevant legislation. The CAP copy advice service can provides guidelines to advertisers about this requirement, but it does not provide legal advice.

The ASA had highlighted the issues which arise under this rule where the products which are advertised are legal to advertise and to buy, but may be illegal to use. Examples would include decoder cards which enable users to receive satellite television channels without paying subscription charges or equipment which enables telephone calls to be intercepted. The ASA had indicated that advertisements for such products should contain a clear and prominent warning of the legal risks to the consumer of using the product. The advertisement must not encourage the use of the product in an illegal way.

Decency

Advertisements should contain nothing that is likely to cause serious or widespread offence. The Code provides that particular care must be taken to avoid causing offence on the grounds of race, religion, sex, sexual orientation or disability.

Compliance with this rule should be judged by considering the advertisement as a whole and the context in which it appears, the sensibilities of its audience, the nature of the product which is being advertised and prevailing standards of decency generally.

The offence caused by the advertisement must be *serious* or *widespread*. The fact that some people find an advertisement offensive will not be sufficient grounds to give rise to a breach of the Codes if the offence caused does not meet these criteria.

What is offensive?

The ASA is charged with assessing whether advertisements are likely to cause serious or widespread offence. It is not current ASA practice to conduct surveys or other research as part of the investigation of specific complaints in order to help the council to reach their decision. The ASA holds regular consumer conferences at which it will try to gauge consumer opinion on topics which are perceived to be sensitive. It also commissions consumer research on a regular basis. These general indications of public attitudes towards particular topics are kept in mind by the ASA when it makes a decision about whether a particular advertisement is sufficiently offensive to be in breach of the Code. There is a wealth of seemingly inconsistent decisions. It may be that in this most subjective of areas the Council would benefit from the use of straw polls to test public reaction to specific advertisements. The use of such procedures might help to build up a body of decisions which could provide useful guidance to those in the industry.

To illustrate the type of inconsistency which exists, set out below are two ASA adjudications from the same monthly report for January 1996 (No 56).

Radio City

Complaints were made about a bus shelter poster advertisement for a radio station featuring a woman wearing a pair of headphones with her eyes closed in obvious enjoyment of whatever she was listening to. The poster featured the caption 'IT'S AURAL SEX'. The complainants objected that the advertisement was in bad taste and offensive.

The complaint was upheld. The ASA considered that the reference to aural sex was an innuendo on oral sex and as such was likely to cause serious or widespread offence.

Compare the decision with the following.

Rogue Golf Company Limited

Complaints were received about an advertisement in a specialist golf magazine for golf clubs. The advertisement featured the head and shoulders of a woman together with a golf club and was captioned 'GREAT HEAD'. The complainants considered that this was a deliberate pun on the act of fellatio and objected that the advertisement was offensive.

The complaint was *not* upheld. The ASA accepted that the advertisement would be understood to be an innuendo as the complainants suggested, but thought that the innuendo was acceptable and would not cause serious or widespread offence.

The decisions are difficult to reconcile. It may be that the ASA was swayed by the fact that the Radio City bus shelter poster would be seen by many people of all ages and outlooks. In contrast, the Rogue Golf Company advertisement, which appeared in a specialist golf magazine, would have an audience which was likely to share a common outlook. It may have been thought that the golfing advertisement was less likely to cause widespread or serious offence amongst this target audience.

The importance of context

Advertisers who place risqué or controversial advertisements in publications which are specifically targeted at a certain type of audience may find that they are given greater leeway by the ASA. This was demonstrated in relation to complaints concerning an advertisement for Benetton Spa which appeared in certain magazines and on a poster. The advertisement featured three hearts with the words white, black and yellow superimposed on each of the respective hearts. The complainants thought that the advertisements were offensive. The complaints were upheld in relation to the poster advertisement on the ground that it was likely to cause serious or widespread offence amongst the general public who were likely to see the poster. The complaints were *not* upheld in relation to the advertisements which appeared in the magazines, because the advertiser and the magazines were able to demonstrate that the likely readers of the publications were young and broadminded and were therefore unlikely to be offended by the imagery.

Products which might be offensive in themselves

The Codes provide that the nature of the product must be taken into account when considering whether an advertisement is offensive. Advertisements may not breach the Code if they are in keeping with the nature of the product that is being advertised, even though they might be thought offensive for other types of product.

When considering a complaint about poster advertisements for Playboy TV which featured a former 'Page 3 girl' wearing lingerie or a short dress under the caption 'KATHY LLOYD PREMIERE ... YOU'LL BE UP ALL NIGHT', the ASA noted that the advertisements were not explicit and reflected the nature of the product. As such they were unlikely to cause widespread or serious offence (*Playboy Television – ASA Monthly Report No 75, August 1997*).

The Playboy decision should be contrasted with a decision in the same monthly report (August 1997) concerning an advertisement for the Bruno Brookes radio show on Aire FM. The poster featured the DJ sitting on a bed fully clothed with a cigar and a drink in his hand. The picture was taken from between the legs of a woman who was wearing stockings and suspenders. The poster featured the caption 'AIRE OF ANTICIPATION!'

A complainant objected that the advertisement was offensive. The ASA upheld the complaint on the ground that the visual was gratuitous and unsuited to the medium chosen (*West Yorkshire Broadcasting plc t/a the New Aire FM – ASA Monthly Report No 75, August 1997*).

In some circumstances, material may not cause serious or widespread offence if it is presented in a light-hearted way so that the audience will see it is a joke. Each case must, however, be considered on its own merits.

Where advertisers realise that their advertisements risk causing offence, they might find it productive to carry out market research to assess public reaction to it before publication. If a complaint is subsequently made about the advertisement, any results from the survey which demonstrate that the advertisement was not thought to be offensive should be shown to the ASA. There are indications in ASA decisions that it will place weight on such evidence where appropriate.

Although most of the published adjudications featuring complaints about decency concern sexual references or inferences, the rule is not restricted to such matters. The depiction of glorified violence has also been found to cause widespread or serious offence. For example, a complaint concerning an advertisement for a computer game which featured violent images such as of a robot with a revolver-like arm holding a severed head on a chain was upheld on the ground that the advertisement was offensive (*Gremlin Interactive Limited – ASA Monthly Report No 73, June 1997*).

The use of or reference to swear words in advertisements is also likely to cause widespread or serious offence.

Example

The ASA objected to a poster for French Connection clothes shops which featured the headline FCUK FASHION. The objection was on the ground that the use of the letters FCUK would be interpreted to be a play on the word 'fuck', even though FCUK was a registered trade mark belonging to the advertiser (*French Connection Group plc – ASA Monthly Report No 74, July 1997*).

Honesty

Advertisers must act responsibly towards consumers. They should not exploit the credulity, lack of knowledge or inexperience of consumers.

Care should be taken when using scientific language or trade jargon where the ordinary consumer would not appreciate its significance or meaning. Where scientific terms are used, their meaning should be clear. Where claims appear in specialist publications, and are therefore likely to be read by specialists in the relevant field, the ASA may take this into account in deciding whether the advertisements will be misleading.

Information of limited value or of questionable validity should not be presented as if it has been universally accepted.

A breach of this rule will almost always be a breach of the rule requiring truthfulness in advertising.

Truthfulness

No advertisement should mislead by inaccuracy, ambiguity, exaggeration, omission or otherwise.

In assessing whether an advertisement is misleading, the *overall impression* of the advertisement must be considered as well as its detailed claims.

Claims can be implied as well as express. Claims can also be made unintentionally.

Example

Complaints were received about a holiday brochure entitled 'Golden Years' which claimed on the front cover that it offered thousands more holidays for the over-50s. The brochure also contained photographs of groups of middle aged and elderly people. The complainant booked one of the holidays, believing from the contents of the brochure that the resort in question would only be for those aged over 50. In fact, the resort was for people of all ages. The complainant objected that the brochure gave a misleading impression.

The advertisers argued that their brochure did not state that the accommodation would be *exclusive* to the older age range. The ASA considered that the photographs in the brochure would give readers the overall impression that the accommodation was exclusively for the over-50s. There was therefore an implied representation to that effect. The complaint was upheld.

The ASA advised the advertisers to include a note in future brochures to explain that the holidays were not age-restricted and also to include representative photographs of a variety of age ranges to avoid giving a misleading impression (*Airtours plc – ASA Monthly Report No 78, November 1997*).

Documentary evidence

Advertisers must hold documentary evidence to prove all claims made in advertisements *before* publication of the advertisements.

Where the claims made are dependent on the individual characteristics of individuals, for example, if the claim concerns the calorie-burning capabilities of a piece of exercise equipment, it should be made clear in the advertisement that the effects of the product will vary from person to person.

Claims for products should, where appropriate, state whether the accuracy of the claims is based on average use and that they may vary if the actual use differs. For example, where a car is advertised with the claim that a major service is required only at intervals of 20,000 miles, the claim should make it clear that the mileage and age of the car, as well as the time which has passed since the last service, would have a bearing on when a major service would be needed (*Volkswagen Group United Kingdom Limited – ASA Monthly Report No 78, November 1997*).

References to tests

Advertisers may wish to refer to tests in their advertisements. If the tests do not originate from within the EU, the advertisement must state that fact. The ASA has shown a tendency to require that tests quoted in advertisements for products in the UK should be carried out with reference to the UK market.

Health claims

Health claims must be fully supported by proper documentary evidence in respect of each specific claim. The claims should be verified by product-specific clinical trials on humans. A claim that a product is beneficial to humans will *not* be proved by tests on the product alone. Where the product makes claims about healthy humans, the tests should be carried out on healthy humans. Where they make claims for particular groups, such as asthma sufferers or arthritis sufferers for example, the tests should be carried out on the relevant groups.

Example

Company X advertises a product which it claims will kill dust mites and will therefore be of benefit to asthma sufferers. The ASA requires X to verify this claim.

(a) In support of its claim, X produces a selection of convincing and scientifically valid research from leading authorities, which demonstrates that when the amount of dust mites in the environment is reduced, the condition of human asthma sufferers tends to improve.

That will not be sufficient. Company X will need to provide the ASA with test results on the product itself.

(b) In support of its claims, X provides the information referred to above *and* the results of tests on its product, which demonstrate that the product reduces the number of dust mites in the environment.

That will still not be sufficient to support the claim that the product has health benefits. Company X will need to produce clinical trials of the efficacy of the product on humans before such a claim can be made.

(c) In support its claims, X conducts clinical trials of the product on human asthma sufferers. The results demonstrate that the product is of benefit to asthma sufferers.

That may be sufficient provided that the trials are scientifically valid. The ASA will reach its decision on this question on the basis of established scientific knowledge. It may consult experts to help it to do so.

The CAP has produced a guidance note on advertisements for asthma and allergy claims, which is available free of charge from the copy advice service.

Small print

Essential information must not be hidden away. Small print should expand on the main theme of the advertisement. It may qualify the theme in the advertisement but it should not contradict the theme. Otherwise the main message of the advertisement would be misleading.

Care should be taken to avoid attention-grabbing headlines, which are then qualified or contradicted in the small print.

Example

Britannia Music Company advertised their music club in inserts to magazines. The insert featured a headline in the following terms: 'TAKE 5 CDs OR CASSETTES AND ONLY PAY FOR 1'. In smaller type, it was made clear that the offer was conditional on the reader buying at least six further albums from the club over the next two years.

The ASA found that the headline gave a false impression. The small print did not qualify the headline. It contradicted it. The complaint was upheld.

The ASA's approach to the interpretation of advertisements

The ASA has a tendency to adopt a restrictive and literal approach to the interpretation of claims made in advertisements.

The Codes contain a provision that allowance should be made for the use of obvious untruths or exaggerations in advertisements which are unlikely to mislead (often called puffery). Puffery is allowed provided that it does not affect the accuracy or perception of the advertisement in any material way. In practice, the ASA makes little allowance for puffery.

Example

Direct Line Insurance plc advertised its insurance products using a poster with the caption 'BEST FOR PRICE. BEST FOR SERVICE'.

A complaint was made about these claims by the British Insurance and Investment Brokers' Association on the ground that Direct Line Insurance was not always best for value. In support of the objection, the complainant produced examples of instances where its members were able to beat Direct Line on price. It also objected to the claim 'best for service' on the ground that a direct insurer, which cuts out middlemen, would not provide the same standard of service as that given by a broker.

Both of the complaints were upheld.

As regards 'BEST FOR PRICE', the ASA considered that readers of the advertisement would infer that the advertisers would *always* offer the cheapest price.

The advertiser sought to show that although sometimes other competitors offered cheaper prices, that did not detract from the claim generally. In support of the claim they produced copies of surveys which had appeared in *Which?* magazine giving the advertisers 'best buy' ratings, sometimes equally with other insurers. The evidence did not satisfy the ASA, which required substantiation of their interpretation of the claim, namely, that in all instances the advertiser offered the best deal.

A similar approach was taken by the ASA in relation to the claim 'BEST FOR SERVICE'. The ASA explains the position as follows:

> ... the way that claims such as 'the best' or 'number one', etc, will depend on how such words are qualified. Claims such as 'best for service' would need to be supported by evidence. Claims which are not qualified, for example, 'simply the best' without any element of comparison are more likely to be seen as expressions of opinion which are unlikely to breach the code.

(*ASA Monthly Report No 85, June 1998*)

The ASA's approach should be contrasted with the way in which the courts interpret advertisements. The reader is referred to Chapters 1, 3 and 8 for an analysis of the court's approach. The court will try to place itself in the position of the reasonable audience and to ask what it would find an advertisement to mean. Allowance would be made for the use of general hyperbole which the reasonable audience would be unlikely to interpret literally.

It is suggested that a court would have found the Direct Line Insurance advertisement to be acceptable on the basis that the statements contained in it were general statements of overall superiority as opposed to literal statements of fact.

Advertisers should bear in mind that the ASA will generally adopt a literal approach to the interpretation of advertisements and that their interpretation must be supported by evidence.

The use of 'leading'

Phrases such as 'The Market Leader' or 'The Leading Manufacturer of ...' or 'Number One for ...' will tend to be construed by the ASA to mean that the advertiser has the largest quantitative share of the market. If the claim is intended to convey that the advertiser is the leader in quality as opposed to quantity, the advertisement should make that clear. In either case, the advertiser should be able to produce evidence to prove the claim.

Matters of opinion

Advertisers may give a view about any matter, including the qualities or desirability of their products, provided that it is clear that they are expressing their own opinion rather than stating a fact. If it is not so clear, or if the statements go beyond the expression of opinion, evidence will be required to substantiate the assertions. It is a question of fact in each case whether an expression is genuinely an opinion or whether it is actually fact dressed up as opinion.

Fear and distress

Advertisers should not use shocking claims or images to attract attention, nor should they play on fear in order to persuade the public to make a purchase. No advertisement should make use of shock tactics which are gratuitous or likely to cause serious or widespread offence or which do not relate to the product/service that is being advertised.

No advertisement should cause fear or distress without good reason. Advertisers may appeal to fear to encourage prudent behaviour or to discourage dangerous or ill-advised actions, but the fear likely to be aroused should not be disproportionate to the risk.

Safety, violence and antisocial behaviour

Advertisements should not show or encourage unsafe practices except in the context of promoting safety. Particular care should be taken with advertisements addressed to or depicting children or young people. Advertisements must not incite the commission of a crime, for example, drinking and driving should not be encouraged.

Advertisements should contain nothing which condones or promotes violence or antisocial behaviour, for example, the depiction of people dropping litter would infringe this provision.

Political advertising

The Code defines political advertising as advertising which concerns party politics, that is, advertisements whose principal function is to influence opinion in favour of or against any political party or candidate contesting a UK or European parliamentary election, a local government election or any matter which is to be decided by the UK electorate by way of referendum.

Such advertising is allowed under the Code. It is *exempt* from certain of the Code rules as follows:

(a) there is no need for the advertiser to hold documentary evidence to support its claims before publication of the advertisement;

(b) there is no requirement for the advertisement to comply with the rule relating to truthfulness;

(c) testimonials may in themselves constitute substantiation of claims in an advertisement;

(d) there is no need for any comparisons to be clear and fair;

(e) political advertisements may attack and denigrate political competitors even though the attacks may be unfair.

All other provisions of the Codes must be complied with.

Advertising by central or local government or concerning government policy does not fall within the definition of political advertising. The Code does therefore apply in full to such advertising, without any exceptions.

There has been recent discussion as to whether political advertising should fall to be regulated by the CAP Codes at all. It may be that the next revision of the Codes will remove such advertising from its remit completely.

Testimonials and endorsements

Testimonials and endorsements in advertisements are permitted, provided that they relate to the product being advertised.

Fictitious endorsements are also permitted, but they must not be represented to be genuine. For example, the use of a testimonial from a fictitious therapist to support health claims for a medical procedure is likely to mislead; particularly if it is used in conjunction with the name of a hospital or a Harley Street address.

A testimonial or an endorsement does not in itself constitute proof or substantiation of the claims made in an advertisement. The testimonial or endorsement must be supported by independent evidence. The fact that a testimonial or an endorsement is presented as an opinion will not save the advertiser from this requirement if the substance of the claim is based in fact.

Example

Objections were received to an advertisement for a health bracelet containing several testimonials about health benefit claims for the bracelet.

The advertiser produced signed and dated copies of the testimonials that showed them to be genuine. The ASA upheld the complaints. Although the testimonials were accepted to be genuine, there was no independent evidence to support the health benefit claims contained in the testimonials. The ASA asked the advertisers not to use the testimonials again (*Carnell Limited – ASA Monthly Report No 77, October 1997*).

Advertisers should not rely solely on testimonials from experts without firstly conducting research to establish that the balance of scientific opinion supports the experts' views.

Advertisers should hold signed and dated proof for any testimonial used, including a contact address for the person in question.

A testimonial should not be used without written permission of the person who gave the testimonial.

Sometimes testimonials refer to tests or trials. Such references are allowed, provided they are made with permission. The reader is referred to the section on truthfulness, p 173, for an explanation of the ASA's practice when considering the adequacy of tests generally.

Care should be taken to ensure that any establishment referred to in the testimonial is *bona fide* and that it is under the direct supervision of an appropriately qualified professional.

Prices

Any stated price should be clear and should relate to the product that is illustrated or referred to in the advertisement.

Example

Complaints were received about an advertisement for a machine tool for a milling machine. The advertisement featured a photograph of the machine tool captioned 'FOR UNDER £40,000'. In fact the particular machine tool that was featured in the picture retailed at considerably more than £40,000. The ASA upheld a complaint that the price quoted did not match the product illustrated (*Mikron (Birmingham) Limited – ASA Monthly Report No 76, September 1997*).

It is not acceptable to feature a top of the range product alongside a bottom of the range price.

Where appropriate, the basis of the price calculation should be included and it should be made clear if the prices quoted are given for guidance only.

Example

An advertisement for cavity wall insulation contained a table that listed five property types with corresponding prices. The table was intended to be a guide to the cost of the insulation. A complainant to the ASA was quoted a higher price than appeared in the advertisement. The higher price arose because the complainant's house had a larger wall space than the house featured in the advertisement. The complaint was upheld on the basis that the prices were not presented as a guide, nor was the basis for the calculation included (*The Energy Saving Trust – ASA Monthly Report No 78, November 1997*).

What about VAT?

The Codes provide that unless advertisements are directed exclusively to the trade, prices quoted should include any VAT payable.

The CAP copy advice team has produced a guidance note offering advice about VAT. The correct presentation of VAT will depend on the readership of the medium in which the advertisement appears, *not* the target audience for the advertisement.

(a) If the medium in which the advertisement appears is read by consumers, the prices shown should normally include VAT.

(b) If the medium is read by the trade and by consumers, it is acceptable to show both VAT inclusive and exclusive prices, but the VAT inclusive price should be given greater prominence.

(c) If the medium is read by the trade and by consumers, but the advertisement features a product or service that will only be of interest to trade readers, the product may be shown as a VAT exclusive price only.

(d) If the medium is read by the trade only, advertisements may quote VAT exclusive prices only.

Where the quoted price is exclusive of other taxes, duties or compulsory charges, the advertisement must make that clear. The amount of any such additional charges should be given where possible.

Price claims should be accurate. Claims such as 'UP TO ...' or 'DISCOUNTS FROM ...' are permissible, provided that the advertisements do not exaggerate the availability of any benefits that are likely to be obtained by consumers.

If the price of one product is dependent on the purchase of another, the extent of any commitment by consumers must be made clear.

Particular guidance regarding compulsory holiday insurance and flight prices

The CAP copy advice team has produced two detailed guidance notes concerning the above matters.

Compulsory holiday insurance

If the holiday which is being advertised is subject to the purchase of compulsory insurance, this should be stated, as should the typical cost of the insurance. The condition must be shown in a way that can easily be seen by the reader. If the cost is shown in a footnote, it must be clearly referable to the cost of the holiday by use of an asterisk.

The advertisement can either give the cost of the holiday plus the cost of insurance, or alternatively it can express the total cost as one figure. If the latter formula is used, the typical cost of the insurance must be set out separately.

Flight prices

If not all flights are available at the quoted fare, advertisements should state prices from the quoted fare of £ ... and that restrictions apply. All flights quoted should be available in sufficient quantities to ensure that consumers have reasonable prospects of obtaining the price that is advertised. The advertisement must clearly indicate if the advertised price excludes compulsory taxes or duties such as airport tax.

All fares quoted should apply to departures on dates within one to six weeks after the advertisement appears. If not, the advertisement must indicate the date(s) on which the flights are available or include some other qualification, for example, Christmas flights.

The price of telephone calls

The price of premium rate calls and of other calls charged at above standard rates should be set out in advertisements or promotions which involve the making of telephone calls.

Free offers

A free offer may be conditional on the purchase of other items. This must, however, be made clear.

An offer should *not* be described as free if consumers pay *more than* the following:

(a) current rates of postage;

(b) actual cost of freight or delivery;

(c) cost of travel if the consumer collects the item.

In particular, where an offer is described as free there should be no additional charge for packing and handling other than those set out above.

An advertisement must make clear whether there is any liability of the consumer for costs *in all material* which refers to the offer. Advertisers must not attempt to recover the cost of free offers by inflating the cost of any product that must be purchased as a precondition of the free offer or by otherwise reducing its quality or composition.

Example

An objection was received to an insert to a holiday brochure advertising a free half day excursion on a particular holiday on the basis that the overall cost of the holiday had been increased to include the excursion. The complaint was upheld. The cost of the holiday was inclusive of the excursion, so it could not properly be described as free (*Travel Clubs International Limited – ASA Monthly Report No 76, September 1997*).

Availability of products

Products must not be advertised unless advertisers can demonstrate that they have reasonable grounds for believing that they can satisfy demand. The demand should be capable of being satisfied at the time that the advertisement is placed. Products must actually be available for dispatch at the time that the advertisement appears. If a product becomes unavailable, advertisers are required to withdraw their advertisement swiftly, wherever possible. In addition to making a reasonable estimate of demand before the advertisement is published, advertisers are required to monitor stock and to communicate with retail outlets to ensure an adequate chain of supply so that demand can be met.

If stocks are limited (for example, where the product advertised is a limited edition), advertisers must make that clear in order to avoid causing unnecessary disappointment.

Switch selling is not permitted. Switch selling takes place when advertisers recommend the purchase of a more expensive alternative to the product advertised, thereby using the advertisement for the lower priced item as a way of generating interest in the more expensive item.

Guarantees

The full term of any guarantee should be available for consumers to inspect before purchase.

Any substantial limitations, such as the need to provide proof of purchase or to use the advertiser's engineers to carry out repairs, should be clearly stated in the advertisement. Advertisers should also inform consumers about how to obtain redress under the guarantee and about the nature and extent of those rights granted by the guarantee which are additional to the rights given to the consumer by law.

Where the product is advertised in a catalogue or a brochure, the statement referring to the above matters should appear beside the product. It will be rarely be sufficient to include the statement elsewhere in the catalogue or brochure or in a different publication such as the product instruction manual.

Identifying advertisers and recognising advertisements

Advertisers, publishers and owners of media are charged with the task of ensuring that advertisements are designed and presented so that they can be easily distinguished from editorial.

THE SALES PROMOTION CODE – A DETAILED EXAMINATION

Preliminary points

The Code applies to the administration of and the rules for sales promotions as well as to the marketing of the promotion.

Primary responsibility for ensuring compliance with the Codes rests with the promoter itself. A close watching brief should therefore be maintained on agencies engaged to devise and administer promotions. Responsibility for compliance with the Codes cannot be abrogated by the engagement of outside professionals. Promoters must be able to demonstrate that they have complied with the Code on request by the ASA by submitting documentary evidence of compliance without delay upon a request being made.

Many of the rules in the Sales Promotion Code are the same as the rules contained in the Advertising Code. Where appropriate, the reader should refer to the relevant section of the Advertising Code for elaboration.

Public interest and legality

Sales promotions should not be designed or conducted in a way that conflicts with the public interest. They should contain nothing that condones or is likely to provoke violent or antisocial behaviour. Promoters have primary responsibility for ensuring that the promotion is legal. Of particular relevance to this obligation will be the requirements of the Lotteries and Amusements Act 1976. That Act is considered in more detail in Chapter 9.

Sales promotions should contain nothing that breaks the law or incites others to break it or omit anything that the law requires.

The reader is referred to the commentary on the legality requirements of the Advertising Code for further detail.

Honesty

Promoters should not abuse consumers' trust or exploit their lack of knowledge or experience.

Truthfulness

No sales promotion should mislead by inaccuracy, ambiguity, exaggeration, omission or otherwise.

Protection of consumers and promoters

(a) Promotions involving dangerous activities should be made as safe as possible by promoters.

(b) Every effort should be made to avoid harming consumers when distributing product samples.

(c) Special care should be taken with regard to promotions addressed to children or where products may fall into the hands of children (even when targeted at adults).

(d) Literature accompanying promotional items should give any necessary safety warnings.

Privacy

Promotions should be designed and conducted in a way that respects the rights of consumers to a reasonable degree of privacy and freedom from annoyance.

Consumers should be told *before entry* if participants may be required to become involved in any of the promoter's publicity (whether connected with the sales promotion or not). Prizewinners should not be compromised by the publication of detailed information about themselves, for example, publication of their home address.

Promoters should ensure that the way they compile and use personal information about consumers conforms to the rules on List and Database Practice, which are contained in the Code.

Suitability

Promoters should make every effort to ensure that unsuitable or inappropriate material does not reach consumers. Neither the sales promotion nor the promotional item should cause offence.

Alcoholic drinks and tobacco products should not feature in sales promotions addressed to people who are under 18.

Tobacco promotions should only be targeted at existing smokers. They should also comply with the detailed rules set out in the Cigarette Code.

Availability

The promoter should be able to demonstrate that it has made a reasonable estimate of likely response and that it is capable of meeting that response at the time that the promotion is launched and throughout its duration. The overriding obligation is to take *reasonable steps* to avoid disappointing consumers. What is reasonable will depend on the facts of each case. Promoters should be able to demonstrate that their estimate of demand is reasonable by showing that it is based on past experience or that it is made in reliance of information furnished by a responsible trade association or a similar third party. Promoters should also be in a position to show that the estimate is current. If there is a delay in launching the promotion, the estimate should be revised.

Where the promotion is for a seasonably variable item such as flights or hotel accommodation, an estimate of demand and capability of meeting the demand may become inaccurate if there is a delay in launching the promotion. The availability of hotel accommodation may be good in the immediate aftermath of Christmas, but become scarcer as Easter approaches, for example.

Phrases such as 'subject to availability' will not exempt the promoter from its obligation to take all reasonable steps to avoid disappointing participants. Where there is limited availability, a disclaimer should alert consumers to the possible restrictions in supply.

Example

Objections were received to a promotion run by HJ Heinz and Company Limited in the form of a direct mail offer with the following headline 'GREAT SOUP GIVEAWAYS. HUNDREDS OF FLASKS AND APRONS FREE WITH HEINZ SOUP LABELS'.

The promotion had a footnote in the following terms: 'This is a limited offer. Applications for the free flasks and aprons will be handled on a first come first served basis until stocks are exhausted.'

The complainants were disappointed applicants who were told that stocks of the flasks and aprons had run out but were not offered an alternative product. They complained that the promotion did not comply with the Code.

Heinz said that they had been overwhelmed by the response to the offer. The ASA found that, even though Heinz had stated that the offer was limited, the statement did not release them from the obligation to take reasonable steps to avoid disappointing consumers. The ASA criticised Heinz' action in telling applicants that they would not get free gifts. In fact Heinz had already obtained more stocks of the aprons and flasks which they planned to send to all disappointed applicants. The ASA welcomed their actions (*HJ Heinz Company Limited – ASA Monthly Report No 73, June 1997*).

If promoters are unable to supply demand for a promotional offer due to a factor beyond their control, for example, because of unexpectedly high demand, products of a similar or greater quality and value *or* a cash payment should normally be substituted.

Care should be taken to ensure that the substitute is of a similar or greater quality and value. Where a promoter tried to substitute the offer of a landscape gardener to perform a health check on applicant's gardens for a gardening book and a packet of seeds, the ASA took the view that that was a breach of the Code on the ground that the substitutes were of a lesser value to the original offer (*The Telegraph Group Limited t/a Daily Telegraph – ASA Monthly Report No 75, August 1997*).

Promoters should ensure that staff on the ground who are responsible for the contact with consumers are adequately briefed about the terms of promotions and availability of relevant stock. The best laid plans can go astray where those implementing them are not aware of all relevant facts.

Example

B&Q advertised a number of products as reduced. A customer tried to buy one of the products, but was told that the product was unavailable in four B&Q stores. He complained to the ASA. B&Q provided stock lists to demonstrate that the product had been in stock at each of the stores at the time of the customer's inquiry. The company was unable to explain why the customer had been given the wrong information. The ASA did not uphold the complaint as it was satisfied that the product was in fact available. It was, however, critical of B&Q's staff and asked the company to ensure that all staff were aware of advertised offers in future.

Participation

Sales promotions should specify how to participate, including any conditions and costs.

Often, the conditions are printed in small type or on the reverse or in a separate document to the teaser for the promotion. This is invariably a breach of the Code. All relevant conditions or restrictions which are likely to affect the consumers' decision to respond or to make a purchase should be clear from the outset. The ASA has stated that readers should not have to scrutinise endless small details in small print before they understand clearly what is on offer. Promoters should not assume that they need not set out conditions in full because the public will realise that they will not get a benefit without something in return.

Examples

Objections were received to an instant win scratchcard that stated that the participant had won a mobile telephone with a free connection *and* a hi fi system. The complainants objected that the promotion did not make clear that it was necessary to subscribe to the advertiser's service and to pay two months' mobile telephone bills to receive the hi fi. The advertisers said that this condition had been made clear on the reverse of the scratchcard. The ASA acknowledged that the rules clarified the offer but was concerned that the clarification was to the opposite effect of the message on the front of the card, namely that the prizes had been won unconditionally. The complaint was upheld (*Odyssey Corporation plc – ASA Monthly Report No 75, August 1997*).

Objections were received to a national press advertisement that offered a free £20 voucher with a mobile telephone and airtime package. The complainants claimed that the advertisement was misleading, because the voucher was given for introducing a friend to the advertiser's service and not just for buying the package.

The advertiser claimed that consumers would understand that the voucher had other conditions attached. The ASA rejected the defence and upheld the complaint (*Dial-a-Phone Limited – ASA Monthly Report No 77, October 1997*).

Other matters that must be set out in the promotion documents are as follows:

(a) The promoter's full name and business address.

(b) A prominent closing date if applicable. If the closing date for purchase of the promoted product is different for the closing date for submission of entries, that should be made clear and both dates should be shown.

(c) Any proof of purchase requirements. The Code provides that this information should be distinguished from the rest of the text, for example, by using bold type or a different colour.

(d) Where it is not obvious, if there is likely to be a limitation on the availability of promotional packs in relation to any stated closing date of the offer.

(e) Where applicable, geographical or personal restrictions should be stated, for example, where tokens were not available in duty free packs of cigarettes (*Imperial Tobacco Limited – ASA Monthly Report No 74, July 1997*).

(f) Where permission is needed from an adult before entry, that fact should be made clear.

(g) Any other factor likely to influence consumers' decisions or understanding about the promotion.

(h) It should be made clear whether any deadline for responding to an undated mailing will be calculated from the date that consumers receive the mailing.

Administration

Sales promotions should be conducted under proper supervision. Adequate resources should be made available to administer them. Promoters and intermediaries should not give consumers any justifiable grounds for complaint.

Promoters should allow ample time for each phase of the promotion.

Promoters should fulfil applications within 30 days unless participants have been informed in advance that it is impractical to do so. The information should usually be set out in the advertisement or promotion itself. Participants should be informed promptly of unforeseen delays in supply and offered an alternative delivery date or a refund.

Where damaged or faulty goods are received, promoters should ensure that they are replaced without cost or that an immediate refund is given. The cost of replacing such goods should fall on the promoter.

If the consumer does not receive goods, the promoter should normally replace them free of charge.

If unwanted mail order goods are returned undamaged within seven working days, the advertiser or promoter should send a full refund to the consumer.

Free offers and promotions where consumers pay

Readers are referred to the section on the Advertising Code for an explanation of the rules relating to free offers. These rules are equally applicable to the Code on sales promotions. In particular, customers should be informed if any conditions apply to the offer.

Example

Objections were received to an in-store promotion stating 'free prescription sunglasses and eye test only £10'. The complainant found the advertisement misleading because it did not make clear that the offer was conditional on the purchase of a pair of prescription glasses. The advertisers said that a footnote to the advertisement instructed customers to ask inside for details. On making such inquiries, customers would at that point be made aware of the full terms of the offer. The ASA did not think that this was clear enough and pointed out that the conditions attaching to the advertisement should be stated in the advertisement itself (*Optical Express Limited – ASA Monthly Report No 77, October 1997*).

Promotions with prizes

The Codes provide that *before* making a purchase, consumers should be provided with the following information about promotions with prizes, which should be prominently shown, for example, in the case of a chocolate bar, on the wrapper itself in such a way that it will be visible before purchase:

(a) the closing date for receipt of entries;

(b) any geographical or personal restrictions such as age;

(c) any requirements for proof of purchase;

(d) the need to obtain permission to enter from an adult or an employer;

(e) the nature of any prizes.

On the last point it is not acceptable to refer to a mystery prize or a prize of value £x, even where the stated value of the prize is accurate. The prizes should always be identified.

Before entry, participants should also be informed of the following:

(a) any restrictions on the number of entries or prizes;

(b) if a cash alternative can be substituted for any prize;

(c) how and when winners will be notified of results;

(d) how and when winners will be announced;

(e) the criteria for judging entries;

(f) where appropriate, who owns copyright in the entries;

(g) whether and how entries will be returned by promoters;

(h) any intention to use winners in post event publicity.

Where prize promotions are widely advertised, promoters should ensure that entry forms and any goods needed to establish proof of purchase are widely available.

The rules

Complex rules should be avoided.

Promoters should not need to supplement conditions of entry with additional rules.

The rules should contain nothing which contradicts the way in which a competition is promoted.

Participants should be able to retain entry instructions and rules.

Closing date

The closing date for entry in a competition should not be changed unless circumstances outside the reasonable control of the promoter make it unavoidable. A poor response or an inferior quality of entries is not sufficient to justify such a change unless the promoter has given prior notice of its intention to extend the life of the promotion in such circumstances.

The closing date for submitting entries should be in keeping with the duration of the competition. For example, a 21 day limit for submission of entries in circumstances where the actual closing date was two years after the mailings were first distributed has been found to be a breach of the Code (*JND Limited – ASA Monthly Report No 73, June 1997*).

The prizes

Promoters must publish or make available on request details of the names and county of major prizewinners and their winning entries.

Unless otherwise stated in advance, prizes should be received no more than six weeks after the promotion has ended.

If the selection of winning entries is open to subjective interpretation, for example, where contestants are asked to complete a slogan or phrase, a competent independent judge or a panel of competent individuals, including at least one member who is independent of the promoter or the promoter's intermediaries, should be appointed.

The identity of the judges should be made available on request.

An independent observer should supervise prize draws to ensure that all participants have an equal opportunity of winning.

Instant win promotions

Promoters should ensure that tokens, tickets or numbers for instant win or other promotions are allocated on a fair and random basis.

Participants should either get their winnings at once or they should be immediately informed that they have won a prize and given details of how to claim it. The claiming of the prize must not involve delay, unreasonable costs or administrative barriers.

Distinction between prizes and gifts

The distinction between items which are available to all entrants and those which are only available to the winners should always be clear to consumers. The two concepts are different and should not be confused. A *gift* is something offered to all participants in a promotion. A *prize* is available only to those who win. A reference to participants *winning awards* is not acceptable where the awards in question are available to all those who entered the competition.

Some promotions have both gifts and prizes. Whilst that is acceptable, care should be taken not to cause confusion between the two.

Exaggeration of the likelihood of winning a prize

One of the more frequent reasons why promotions fall foul of the Code is that they exaggerate the likelihood of contestants winning a prize. Prominent headlines often give the impression that a consumer has already won a prize. On reading the small print the consumer then finds that that is not the case. Alternatively, the impression might be given that the consumer has won a major prize when only a small prize has been awarded to him/her. Both of these scenarios will involve a breach of the Code.

Promotions should be distinguishable

Advertisement promotions should be designed and presented in such a way that they can be easily distinguished from editorial.

Front page flashes

Publishers announcing reader promotions on the front page or cover of newspapers and magazines should ensure that consumers know whether they will be expected to buy subsequent editions of the publication to benefit from the promotion. Major qualifications that may influence consumers significantly in their decision to purchase the publication should also appear on the front page or the cover.

The CAP has issued a guidance note on front page flashes. It contains the following advice.

Token promotions

Some promotions require that tokens or vouchers be collected over a period of time. Often this requirement is not set out on the cover of the publication. The ASA has consistently regarded the omission of this condition as something that would be likely to influence consumers significantly in their decision to purchase. The Help Note suggests that front page flashes should avoid the implication that the promotion or competition can be entered into with the purchase of only one edition of the publication if that is not the case. Statements such as 'starts/continues today' or 'first/second token inside' should be used to prevent confusion arising.

Conditional purchase promotions

Conditional purchase promotions require that the offer must be redeemed from one specific company or outlet or that the offer is conditional on the purchase of another item, for example, a free drink when you purchase a burger.

All such conditions should be made clear in the flash. The conditions should ideally be spelt out. The failure to do so is invariably regarded by the ASA to be a factor that would influence consumers significantly in their decision to purchase.

Geographical conditions

If readers in some regions cannot participate in the competition or promotion, the flash should make that clear.

Where an offer can only be redeemed in specific outlets and it is known that the number of outlets is limited or non-existent in a particular region, the CAP suggest that copy advice is taken.

'Free inside' promotions

Front page flashes should not give the impression that the items on offer as being free are inside the newspaper or magazine when they are not. Where the offer is a 'mail in' offer, that fact should be made clear. Where it is obvious that the item in question could not be contained in the publication, for example, because of its bulk, then no clarification will be necessary. The expression FREE ... FOR EVERY READER should be avoided where the offer is limited to one gift per household.

Telephone entry

Where offers require participation by way of a telephone call this requirement should be made clear in the flash. The cost of the call should also be made clear.

In the case of free offers, the CAP Help Note states that it is not necessary to state the need for a telephone call, although the reason for the advice is not given. It is recommended that the fact that a call has to be made to claim the offer should always be made clear.

Front page teasers

Front page teasers are forerunners of the promotion. They should not give the misleading impression that the offer starts in that particular edition of the publication.

Charity linked promotions

Advertisements or promotions that claim an association with a charity or a good cause must not be run without the consent of the charity or good cause.

Promotions which claim that participation will benefit charities or is otherwise associated with charities should name each charity or good cause which will benefit.

The benefit to the charity or cause should not be exaggerated. The promoter should be able to make available to consumers on request a current or final total for contributions made.

Where the good cause is not a registered charity, its nature and objectives should be defined in the promotion.

Trade incentives

Trade incentive schemes fall within the ambit of the Code.

A trade incentive scheme should be designed and implemented to take account of the interests of everyone involved. The scheme should not compromise the obligation of employees to give honest advice to consumers.

The promoter should obtain the prior agreement of employers whose employees are participating in the scheme where the incentives are specifically offered to those employees. Where the incentive is generally advertised, employees should be requested to seek permission from their employer before participating.

It should be made clear to those benefiting from an incentive scheme that they may be liable for tax on the benefits that accrue to them.

Advertising and promoting to children

The rules considered above apply equally to advertisements and promotions aimed at or featuring children. The Codes emphasise certain matters as follows.

Advertisements or promotions addressed to or featuring children should contain nothing likely to result in their physical, mental or moral harm, for example, they should not be encouraged to copy any practice that might be unsafe for a child.

Advertisements or promotions should not exploit children's credulity, sense of loyalty, vulnerability or lack of experience.

Children should not be made to feel inferior or unpopular for not buying the advertised product, nor should advertisements actively encourage children to make a nuisance of themselves to parents or others – so called pester power.

It should be made clear that parental permission should be obtained before children are committed to purchasing complex and costly goods and services or where prizes and incentives might cause conflict between children and their parents.

Other specific rules

The Codes contain specific rules that govern advertisements or promotions for the following products:

(a) alcoholic drinks (defined as those exceeding 1.2% alcohol by volume);

(b) motoring;

(c) environmental claims;

(d) health and beauty products and therapies;

(e) medicines;

(f) vitamins, minerals and food supplements;

(g) cosmetics;

(h) hair and scalp products;

(i) slimming products;

(j) financial services and products;

(k) distance selling;

(l) employment and business opportunities.

There are also rules concerning list and database practice, which are beyond the scope of this book.

The Cigarette Code

The Cigarette Code runs parallel to the Codes on advertising and sales promotion and its rules are *additional to* those Codes. Like the other CAP Codes, it applies to non-broadcast advertising. There is a mandatory requirement that cigarette advertisements are pre-cleared through the CAP. Clearance will not protect advertisements from complaints being upheld under the Codes. As with the other Codes, the ASA is the final arbiter on the meaning of the Code's rules.

The Cigarette Code applies to the following:

(a) cigarettes;

(b) tobacco (although the Code does *not* apply to pipe tobacco);

(c) cigarette papers, filters and wrappings;

(d) any advertisement that features a cigarette or a pack design of a recognisable brand in the UK;

(e) advertisements for products displaying the colours, livery, insignia or name of a cigarette brand in a way that promotes smoking;

(f) special offers, competitions and other sales promotions and teasers.

The Cigarette Code does *not* cover the following: cigars, cheroots, cigarillos, snuff or pipe tobacco. Nor does it cover herbal cigarettes or herbal tobaccos. Similarly, cigarette holders, matches, lighters, etc, are not covered unless they fall within the above provisions. Advertisements for cigarettes, etc, which are addressed to the tobacco trade and which appear in media which are not targeted at the public are not governed by the Cigarette Code.

Events that are sponsored by cigarette companies are not covered by the Code.

THE COMPLAINTS PROCEDURE

The ASA responds to complaints received. It can also act on advertisements on its own initiative.

The general procedure is as follows:

(a) A complaint is received and acknowledged by the ASA. Complaints should be in writing and should be accompanied by a copy of the advertisement (or details of where and when it appeared) and as much detail as possible. There is no charge for making a complaint.

(b) The ASA secretariat carries out an initial assessment of the complaint to decide if it should be pursued by the ASA or whether it falls within the remit of another body. If there is obviously no case to answer, the ASA will inform the recipient. If the complaint is already the subject of legal action, the ASA will decline jurisdiction. If it is decided that the case should be pursued, a decision is made as to the way in which it should be investigated.

(c) When the assessment is complete, the secretariat will notify the complainant of the steps it is taking.

(d) The ASA secretariat will then ask the advertiser or promoter to respond to the complaint. Usually, it will ask the advertiser/promoter to address particularly the pertinent issues raised by the complaint by spelling out what they are. It will include the relevant parts of the Codes to assist the advertiser to prepare its response. The advertiser/promoter will be asked to supply evidence to support any disputed claims contained in the advertisement.

(e) The advertiser/promoter should respond in writing. The response should be sent promptly. A response is usually requested by the ASA secretariat within seven days. The Codes require that advertisers/promoters should have evidence to support the truth of factual claims before publication and that they should make it available to the ASA on request without delay. A plea for an extension of time to compile information is unlikely to be treated sympathetically. Any unreasonable delay in responding to the complaint may in itself be a breach of the Codes.

(f) The advertisement/promotion can generally continue to run until the outcome of the complaint. However, where there is an unreasonable delay in responding to the complaint, or where the case seems particularly serious, advertisers may be asked to stop making the disputed claim until a decision is reached.

(g) At the same time as the advertiser/promoter is notified of the complaint, the ASA secretariat will also notify relevant media organisations and publishers that a complaint has been made and how it will be pursued.

(h) The identity of members of the public who make a complaint is not revealed to the advertiser/promoter. The identity of industry complainants, such as trade competitors and other non-private complainants, are disclosed to the advertiser and set out in the ASA Monthly Reports.

(i) When the response is received from the advertiser/promoter, the ASA secretariat will, where necessary, continue to press for further information such as independent expert advice, so that the ASA Council will have adequate material on which to make its adjudication.

(j) The advertisement is then assessed in the light of all the information compiled and the secretariat will prepare a recommendation to the ASA Council. This is also sent to the advertiser/promoter for their comments on its factual accuracy, which must be provided within seven days.

(k) The ASA Council, which consists of a majority of non-industry representatives, considers the complaint and all supporting documents. There are no oral hearings. The ASA considers the complaint on the basis of written representations only. It is not Council practice to allow product demonstrations.

(l) The Council may accept the recommendation of the secretariat or it may amend it or change it completely. The Council is solely responsible for its decision.

(m) The complainant and the advertiser/promoter are informed of the Council's decision. Where the complaint is upheld, the advertiser/promoter will be asked to withdraw or amend the advertisement.

(n) The outcome of the complaint is published in the *ASA Monthly Reports*.

(o) The ASA will check whether its decision has been complied with.

(p) Appeals can be made to the ASA Chairman. Any appeal must be accompanied by new evidence or should demonstrate a substantial flaw in the conclusion reached by the ASA Council. The appeal should be in writing and be signed by the chief executive of the advertiser/promoter.

(q) The making of an appeal will not delay the inclusion of the original decision in the ASA Monthly Report. If the appeal is successful, the revised decision will be printed in a later report.

(r) There is no further right of appeal against an ASA decision.

The decision of the ASA can be challenged in the courts by way of an application for judicial review. Under the judicial review process, the court will not substitute its own decision for that of the ASA. Instead, it will consider whether the ASA reached its decision in a reasonable manner, for example, by considering all the relevant evidence. If it decides that the ASA acted unreasonably, the court will order it to reconsider its decision. The court will not substitute its decision for that of the ASA. The manner in which the decision is arrived at may change, but the actual decision may not.

Recently, Direct Line Financial Services Limited applied for a decision of the ASA Council to be reviewed by the court. It also obtained an order that during the interim period until the court reached its decision on the judicial review application, the Council decision should not appear in the *ASA Monthly Report* – in effect, putting a temporary embargo on the publication of the decision. The writer believes that this was the first time that an applicant for judicial review has obtained such an order.

The reader is referred to Chapter 15 for further details about judicial review.

CHAPTER 18

THE INDEPENDENT TELEVISION COMMISSION CODES OF ADVERTISING STANDARDS AND PRACTICE AND PROGRAMME SPONSORSHIP

THE CODES

The Independent Television Commission (ITC) is a statutory body which regulates commercial television companies in the UK. Aside from its regulatory function, it also awards broadcasting licences to television companies. Its licensees consist of all the UK terrestrial and cable television companies and satellite services which operate from the UK.

One of the duties imposed on the ITC is the drawing up and enforcement of Codes governing standards and practice in television advertising and programme sponsorship. The ITC has promulgated two Codes, respectively:

(a) the Code of Advertising Standards and Practice; and

(b) the Code of Programme Sponsorship.

Both of those Codes will be considered in this chapter. They apply to all the television companies that are licensed by the ITC.

Complaints about advertisements are considered by the ITC, which publishes regular reports setting out details of all complaints of substance which have been considered. Unfavourable decisions are likely to attract adverse publicity for the advertiser.

The authority of the ITC

The ITC has authority over its licensees rather than over individual advertisers. All holders of ITC licences are required to ensure that the advertising which they broadcast complies with the Codes. Broadcasters are directly responsible for the advertisements which they transmit and the ITC can require broadcasters to withdraw advertising which does not comply with the Codes. Such a requirement will be mandatory and will have immediate effect. The end result is harmful to the advertiser, who will find that his advertising is denied a broadcast outlet.

Television companies can be subject to severe sanctions for non-compliance with ITC decisions, including large fines and ultimately revocation of their licences.

Appeals to the court from adverse ITC decisions

The decisions of the ITC can be reviewed by the courts by way of judicial review. The limitations of, and the procedure for, judicial review are considered in Chapter 15. There is no other right of appeal to the courts.

The way that the Codes work in practice

In practice, the advertisers liaise with broadcasters about the content of advertisements. The broadcasters are required by the ITC to have procedures in place to ensure compliance with the Codes. The ITC provides advice to broadcasters about the Codes. Advertisers who require advice about the Codes in relation to specific advertisements should contact the broadcasters or their representatives rather than the ITC.

Most television companies require the advertising which they carry on a national basis to be cleared by the Broadcast Advertising Clearance Centre (BACC). This is an organisation set up and funded by the participating broadcasters. It provides pre-transmission clearance services for ITV, GMTV, Channel 4, Channel 5, BSkyB and UK Gold amongst others. Not all television companies use the BACC for advertising clearance. Some will clear advertisements themselves.

Pre-transmission clearance by or behalf of television companies is, in practice, a mandatory requirement.

Clearance procedures

The clearance requirements and procedures of individual television companies will differ. The BACC's procedure is described below. Whatever the procedure, it is advisable to submit material for clearance at an early stage, ideally at pre-production script stage before filming begins. This will avoid unnecessary expense on filming if the basic concept of the advertisement is flawed. The BACC asks for submission of scripts for proposed advertisements prior to filming.

The BACC clearance practices

Agencies should ideally send pre-production scripts for advertisements to the BACC for its initial examination. Where amendments are required by the BACC to ensure compliance with the Codes, the BACC will discuss them with the agency so that a revised script can be agreed. Where appropriate, the

BACC will offer guidance about the visual content of the advertisements at this preliminary stage. Where matters of taste are involved, advertisers may find that it is cost effective to submit a storyboard or other visual device to the BACC at an early stage.

The BACC will view videotape of the filmed commercial to check that it is in line with the approved script (where there is one) and the Codes.

Where an advertisement contains factual claims, advertisers *must* submit supporting evidence with the script or videotape of the advertisement. Technical or scientific claims will be sent to BACC appointed experts for evaluation.

Sometimes, the BACC will recommend scheduling restrictions for advertisements, for example, that they should not be broadcast in breaks in or around children's programming.

All material submitted to the BACC is submitted in the strictest confidence.

The BACC has produced guidance notes on the precise requirements for material submitted to it for clearance. They are available from the BACC.

Limitations of BACC clearance

The BACC advises under the Codes. Its staff are not legal advisers. Advertisers or television companies seeking advice on the law should consult their own lawyers. Clearance by the BACC will not mean that the advertisement is not an infringement of a third party's rights.

Clearance by the BACC will also be no guarantee that the advertisement complies with the Codes. The ITC sometimes decides that advertisements which the BACC have cleared are in fact in contravention of the Codes.

The above points also apply to clearance by television companies.

Clearance by television companies or the BACC will not guarantee that the commercials will be shown. Broadcasters have a discretion to decline to broadcast advertisements, although the discretion must not be exercised in a way that will unreasonably discriminate in favour of or against a particular advertiser.

This book does not deal in detail with rules governing the scheduling of advertisements. Advertisers should be aware that such rules do exist.

THE ITC CODE OF ADVERTISING STANDARDS AND PRACTICE

General principles

The Code sets out four general principles which should be read in conjunction with the Code's more detailed provisions. They are as follows:

(a) television advertising should be legal, decent, honest and truthful;

(b) advertisements must comply in every respect with the law, common or statute, and licensees must make it a condition of acceptance that advertisements do so comply;

(c) the detailed rules set out in the Code are intended to apply in their spirit as well as their letter;

(d) the standards in the Code apply to any item of publicity inserted in breaks or between programmes, whether in return for payment or not, including publicity by licensees themselves.

The detailed rules

The rules relating to the use of individuals in advertising and the making of comparisons are explained in Chapters 10 and 8 respectively.

Separation of advertisements and programmes

Advertisements (other than those by television companies for programme promotion) must be distinguishable from programmes.

Advertisements should avoid referring to themselves as programmes. The inclusion of extracts from recent programme material should also be avoided, unless it is used in connection with products which are associated with the programme shown, for example, an associated book or video.

Parodies of programmes

Advertisements which parody programmes are permissible provided that they are clearly recognisable as parodies. In order to avoid confusion, parodies should not use the same performers who appeared in the programme which is being parodied. Direct imitations of programmes are not permitted. Compliance with this rule is a question of degree. The line between direct imitation and parody is a fine one. Where appropriate, advertisements should be labelled as advertisements to minimise any risk of confusion. Borderline advertisements may be cleared with scheduling restrictions, to ensure that they cannot be shown around the programme in question.

The BACC requires that permission be obtained from the broadcaster of the programme which is the subject of the parody together with permission from all other relevant rights owners.

Programme performers

This rule applies to performers who appear in television programmes. The appearance of such performers in advertisements could lead to the blurring of the distinction between advertisements and programmes.

The Code permits the use of such performers subject to the preceding rule about the separation of programmes and advertisements being clearly maintained. Advertisements which feature the programme performer will not generally be scheduled in or around the programme in which the performer appears. More stringent timing restrictions may be imposed where appropriate by the BACC, the television company concerned or by the ITC. Performers will not generally be allowed to appear in advertisements in the role of the character which they play in television programmes.

Certain types of people should *never* be used in television advertising (whether in the visuals or to do voice-overs). They are:

(a) Newsreaders appearing on UK television channels, including the BBC (which is not regulated by the ITC).

(b) Persons who regularly present current affairs programmes on UK channels.

(c) Persons who appear regularly in any advisory programmes or in an advisory capacity in any programme on any UK channel where the programme or advice is related to the product being advertised.

Even when presenters/newsreaders have ceased to appear on programmes, they will not be immediately acceptable as performers in advertisements. What the BACC terms 'a period of insulation' will be required. The length of the period will depend on the particular facts.

Subliminal advertising

Advertising which seeks to convey a message to or influence the minds of the audience without their being fully aware of it is not permitted under the Codes. Subliminal messages are also illegal pursuant to s 6(1)(e) of the Broadcasting Act 1990.

Captions and superimposed text

The text of words or captions superimposed on the screen must be clearly legible and must appear on the screen for a sufficient period of time to enable it to be read by the average viewer on a standard television set. The ITC have issued a guidance note on on-screen text and subtitling which provides technical guidance on the requirements of the Codes.

The content of captions and text may qualify or clarify a claim made in the advertisement, but it must *not* contradict the claim.

Noise and stridency

Advertisements should not be excessively noisy or strident.

Politics, industrial and political controversy

Advertisements by or on behalf of any body whose objects are wholly or mainly of a political nature are not permitted under the Codes. 'Political' means more than party politics. It is defined in the Code to mean 'an advertisement intended to change or influence public or government opinion with a view to securing legislative action'. The ITC has a wide discretion to determine what is 'political' for the purposes of the Codes. In a case involving a decision of the ITC's sister regulator in the field of commercial radio, the Radio Authority, the court held that the Radio Authority had not acted unreasonably in disallowing an advertisement by Amnesty International (British section) which drew attention to the breaches of human rights that were then taking place in Rwanda and Burundi. The court was of the view that such an advertisement might reasonably be considered to be political (*R v Radio Authority ex p Bull and Another* [1995] 4 All ER 481).

Where advertisements refer to matters of political or industrial controversy or which relate to public policy, they should be impartial.

Taste and offence

No advertisement should offend against good taste or decency or be offensive to public feeling. No advertisement should prejudice respect for public decency.

The sensitivities of all sections of the viewing audience must be taken into account in determining whether an advertisement complies with this rule. The Code states that care should be taken to avoid stereotyped imagery which might be hurtful to certain sections of the audience, for example, the portrayal of women as sex objects or the use of racial or ethnic stereotypes. The BACC recommends that particular care should be taken in portraying the following:

(a) *Crime, death and violence* – the portrayal of serious violence should be avoided. Depending on the context, humorous representations of violence may be permissible. References to suicide or attempted suicide should be avoided. The humorous treatment of death or serious injuries should also be avoided. The depiction of *non-violent* crime can be permissible but not in a way which appears to condone or trivialise such crime. The BACC advises that an indication that a perpetrator of non-violent crimes has been, or will shortly be, caught should be included in the advertisement, for example, the sound of police sirens as the perpetrator is shown to be committing his crimes.

(b) *Good manners and behaviour* – advertisements should not portray antisocial or irresponsible behaviour or the lack of reasonable courtesy, for example, queue jumping, the dropping of litter on the floor, road rage. Children should not be shown as being engaged or about to be engaged in serious mischief. Behaviour prejudicial to the environment should not be portrayed in a way which appears to condone it (although this rule does not extend to advertisements for products/services which may have an adverse effect on the environment in normal everyday use, for example, cars).

(c) *Safety* – advertisements should not include anything likely to encourage dangerous or harmful conduct or behaviour prejudicial to health and safety, for example, depicting people travelling in a car as not wearing seat belts or a person crossing a road without first checking whether it is safe to cross.

Fear and superstition

Advertisements must not play on fear or exploit the superstitious.

Driving

Advertisements should not encourage or condone dangerous, inconsiderate or competitive driving practices or breaches of the Highway Code.

In relation to advertisements for motor vehicles, references to power or acceleration should not imply that speed limits might be exceeded. The BACC suggests that top speed capabilities in excess of the speed limit should not be given. There must be no suggestion of excitement or aggression accompanying the reference to speed. The depiction of car chases is unlikely to be acceptable.

Misleadingness

The ITC is required by the Control of Misleading Advertisements Regulations 1988 (as amended by the Broadcasting Act 1990) to investigate complaints about misleading advertising. The reader is referred to Chapter 7 for further information about the regulations.

The Code provides that the television companies must satisfy themselves that the advertiser has substantiated claims and illustrations before the advertisements can be accepted for broadcast. Health claims require particularly close scrutiny for any type of product.

Advertisements should contain no descriptions, claims or illustrations which are either expressly or impliedly misleading about the product/service advertised or its suitability for the recommended purpose. Care should be taken over phrases such as 'the Number 1 Product of this Type' or 'Unbeatable Value'. The television companies, or ultimately the ITC, are likely to require substantiation of such claims.

In practice, all claims (whether express or implied) must be supported by verifiable evidence before broadcast. If supporting evidence is unavailable, the advertisements will *not* be acceptable for broadcast. Where appropriate, the television companies/the BACC will ask independent experts to assess scientific or technical evidence which is submitted by advertisers for consideration.

Advertisements must not exploit public ignorance by the use of scientific jargon or terminology which will be unfamiliar to the layperson. Claims should not be made to look as if they have a scientific basis when they do not. Claims of a limited validity should not be couched in such a way to make them seem to be of universal validity.

Where claims are subject to important qualifications or limitations then details of them must be given.

Price claims

Price claims must comply with the Consumer Protection Act 1987 (see Chapter 6 for further details). Where the advertisement is for mail order goods, postage and packing charges should be stated. The omission of such information will render the advertisement misleading.

Testimonials

The BACC defines testimonials to mean expressions of opinion or statements of experience from a real person.

The use of testimonials is permitted subject to the matters set out below.

Testimonials must be genuine and must not be used in a manner likely to mislead. Television companies must seek and obtain satisfactory documentary evidence in support of any testimonial *and of the claims contained in the testimonial* before accepting any relevant advertisement.

Testimonials should not be presented in a way which would lead the viewer to believe that the testimonial is a factual claim when it is only a subjective statement. The use of phrases such as '*In my opinion* this floor cleaner is superior to all others on the market' or '*I have found* that no other soap powder keeps my whites looking whiter' will help to stress that the testimonial is subjective.

Testimonials must be up to date in the sense that they must relate to the current characteristics of the product/service that is available on the market. The BACC requires that testimonials must not be more than three years old.

Actors should not be used to stand in for the actual people who have given their testimony, although actors can give their own testimony.

Testimonies should not be given in return for payment. Where the individual is asked by the advertiser to try out the product/service for payment, the advertisement should make the fact of the request clear. The BACC suggests the following type of formula: 'X Limited asked me to try out this new toothpaste and it tastes really good.'

Testimonials – remuneration

The BACC guidance notes state that well known personalities may receive a fee in return for their association with particular products. Remuneration paid to other types of people should be restricted to reimbursement of reasonable expenses and a nominal reward.

Testimonials – documentary evidence

The BACC requires that the following evidence in support of any testimony be produced to it:

(a) A signed and witnessed confirmation by the testifier that the statement made by him or her or about him or her which appears in the advertisement is true and accurate and (except where the advertisement indicates otherwise) that the views or matters expressed were formed or occurred independently of any approach from the advertiser.

(b) A signed confirmation from the advertiser that to the best of its knowledge and belief the testimony given is genuine and that the BACC's requirements have been complied with (see above).

(c) Confirmation that the testifier appearing in the advertisement is not an actor or model (unless indicated in the advertisement that the views expressed are those of the actor/model).

(d) The original or photocopies of any document quoted from or referred to.

Children should not be used to give formal testimonies, although it is permissible to show them giving spontaneous comments on matters in which they would have an obvious natural interest.

Trade approvals and recommendations

Trade approvals, endorsements and recommendations are permitted in principle, provided that they are genuine and do not mislead. The BACC point out that words such as 'as recommended by' or 'as chosen by' should be used with caution, as they imply that the company making the endorsement would exclusively use the products/services. Such words should be avoided where no exclusivity in fact exists.

Guarantees

The words 'guarantee', 'guaranteed' and ' warranty' or words with a similar meaning should not be used *unless* the full terms of the guarantee, etc, are available for inspection by the television company concerned. The terms must also be set out clearly in the advertisement or otherwise made available to the purchaser of the goods/services in writing either at the point of sale or with the goods/services. The terms must include details of the remedial actions under the guarantee/warranty, which are available to the purchaser.

Use of the word 'free'

Goods/services should not be described as 'free' unless they are supplied at no cost other than actual postage or carriage charge or incidental travelling costs incurred by the customer in collecting the offer. No extra charge for handling or packing is permissible.

Competitions

Advertisements featuring competitions are permissible provided that they comply with the Lotteries and Amusements Act 1976 (except in Northern Ireland where the Act does not apply). The reader should see Chapter 9 for an explanation of the Act's provisions. Arrangements must be in place to enable prospective participants to obtain printed details of the conditions governing the competition, the rules, and the arrangements for the distribution of prizes and the announcement of results. Any special conditions for entry (for example, it is only open to over 18s) should be given in the advertisement. The value of any prizes and the chances of winning should not be exaggerated.

Mail order and direct response advertising

Advertisements for goods available by mail order or direct response (for example, telephone orders) are permitted subject to the following provisions.

Where the advertiser's full name and address is not given in the advertisement, arrangements must be in place to inform any person who requests these details *from the television company* of those details. The address should be a postal address and should be sufficiently full to enable the advertiser to be located.

The television company/BACC must also be satisfied of the following matters:

(a) Adequate arrangements exist at the address in question during normal office hours to handle any inquiries which may arise from the advertisement.

(b) Samples of the goods advertised are available for public inspection.

(c) The goods dispatched are at all times and in all material respects the same as those shown in the advertisement.

(d) The advertiser is able to meet any reasonably foreseeable demand created by the advertising.

(e) The advertiser is able to fulfil orders within 28 days from receipt (unless there is a satisfactory reason why the delivery period should be longer than 28 days).

(f) Adequate arrangements have been taken for the protection of customers' money.

(g) An undertaking has been received from the advertiser that money will be refunded promptly and in full to buyers who can show justifiable cause for dissatisfaction with the product/service or delay in delivery.

(h) Advertisers must be prepared to demonstrate or supply samples of the product/service being advertised to the television company/the BACC so that they can assess the claims made in the advertising.

(i) Where the advertiser intends to send a representative to call on persons responding to the advertisement, that should be made clear in the advertisement or in the particulars subsequently supplied by the advertiser. The customer must be given an opportunity to refuse any call. The television company/the BACC must obtain adequate assurances that the representative will demonstrate and make available the product type advertised and will not engage in 'switch selling'.

(j) Assurances must be obtained that the advertisers' records of respondents comply with relevant data protection legislation.

Direct response advertising which invites children to purchase products is not permitted.

Home shopping features

Home shopping features of programme length in which goods/services are demonstrated and offered for sale or hire to viewers, are advertisements for the purposes of the Codes and must comply with its rules.

Premium rate telephone services

Regard should be had to the ICSTIS Code for general provisions about advertising premium rate telephone services. Where services lasting longer than five minutes (excluding chat services) are advertised on television, the ITC Code provides that a warning to that effect must be given in the advertisement.

Products/services which cannot be advertised on television

Advertisements for the following products/services or for other products or services which would indirectly publicise the following products/services are unacceptable:

(a) all tobacco products;

(b) pornography;

(c) breath testing devices and products that purport to mask the effect of alcohol;

(d) the occult;

(e) betting tips;

(f) betting and gaming (except football pools and certain lotteries);

(g) private investigation services;

(h) guns and gun clubs;

(i) commercial services offering advice on personal or consumer problems.

Rules for particular situations

In addition to the general rules discussed above, the Code contains detailed rules applicable to the following:

(a) advertising and children;

(b) alcoholic drink;

(c) lotteries and pools;

(d) financial advertising;

(e) medicines, treatments, health claims, nutrition and dietary supplements;

(f) the use of animals in advertisements;

(g) homework schemes;

(h) matrimonial and introduction agencies;

(i) charity advertising;

(j) religious advertising.

THE ITC CODE OF PROGRAMME SPONSORSHIP

The Programme Sponsorship Code is concerned with advertiser involvement in *programming* rather than *advertising* time.

A programme is sponsored for the purposes of the Code if any part of its production or transmission costs are paid by the advertiser with a view to promoting its own or another's name, trade mark, image, activities, products or other direct or indirect commercial interests.

Sponsorship of programmes is permitted subject to the provisions of the Sponsorship Code and the Code on Advertising Standards.

The following bodies cannot sponsor programmes:

(a) political interests (the reader is referred to the discussion of the meaning of 'political' in relation to the ITC Advertising Code, above, p 204);

(b) tobacco manufacturers and producers;

(c) pharmaceutical businesses;

(d) other prohibited advertisers (the reader is referred to the list of prohibited advertisers on p 210).

Bookmaking and gaming businesses may sponsor certain programmes subject to restrictions.

Unsponsorable programmes

The following programmes are unsponsorable:

(a) general news programmes. This does not include certain news-type items which fall outside the context of a general news programme, for example, traffic reports or weather reports;

(b) business and financial reports;

(c) current affairs.

Certain other types of programme are restricted. These are as follows:

(a) consumer advice programmes. They may not be sponsored by advertisers whose business involves the marketing or provision of products/services of the type featured;

(b) programmes dealing with issues about which there is significant public controversy may not be sponsored by an advertiser with a direct interest in the controversy.

The fact of sponsorship must be clear

Sponsorship must be clearly identified at the beginning and/or end of the programme. Credits may also appear when entering/leaving a commercial break. The credits can be aural and/or visual.

The front credit or, where there is none, the end credit should identify the sponsor and explain its relationship to the programme, for example, 'sponsored by' or 'in association with'. Expressions which would suggest that the sponsor is involved in the actual broadcast, for example, 'brought to you by', are not permitted. The credit can indicate the connection between the sponsor and a brand or the nature of the sponsor's business, for example, 'sponsored by X, makers of brand Y' or 'sponsored by Z, makers of biscuits'. The credits can also include a strapline about the sponsor or its products. It must be of a general nature and can take the form of an advertising slogan which is used by the sponsor. It must not however directly encourage the purchase or rental of the sponsor's goods/services, for example, by mentioning particular attributes of the product or services in question. Specific branded product representations are not permitted, nor are extracts from or imitations of the sponsor's advertising campaigns. Trade marks and logos can be included in the credits, as can animation and musical effects. Trailers may refer to the sponsor by way of a single reference of not more than five seconds.

Programme support material such as internet web sites or pamphlets may be sponsored. The sponsor must be identified when details of the ways to obtain the support material are given. A brief visual display of the sponsor's logo and trade mark may be included with the sponsor's name.

Sponsors' names may not be included in the programme title (except where the title is a sponsored event, for example, the Coca Cola Cup Final).

Sponsors are not permitted to influence the content or scheduling of any programme in such a way as to affect editorial independence and the responsibility of the broadcaster. Sponsors should not be referred to in the programmes which they sponsor – although this rule may be relaxed to some degree in relation to single interest channels (for example, travel channels with programmes sponsored by X tourist authority), provided that the programmes do not directly encourage the purchase or rental of the sponsor's product/service.

Other promotional references

Game shows (whether sponsored or not)

Companies can donate their own products as prizes. There can be up to two mentions of the brand of the main prize or prize donor. Product descriptions should not consist of promotional statements.

Viewers competitions

Companies may donate their own products as prizes. There may be a single mention of the brand of the main prize or prize donor. Product descriptions should not consist of promotional statements. Sponsors may *not* donate their own products as prizes in viewers competitions forming part of the programmes which they are sponsoring.

Product placement

Product placement is the practice whereby advertisers secure the inclusion of or reference to their products/services within a programme in return for payment or other valuable consideration. *It is prohibited.*

CHAPTER 19

THE RADIO AUTHORITY ADVERTISING AND SPONSORSHIP CODE

The Radio Authority Code ('the Code') is in many respects similar to the ITC Codes. Readers should therefore cross-refer to Chapter 18. Differences between the requirements of the two sets of Codes will be highlighted in this chapter. This book does not deal in detail with the scheduling provisions of the Code.

The role of the Radio Authority

The Radio Authority is the body which licenses and regulates the independent (that is, non-BBC) radio industry in the UK. Its authority is derived from the Broadcasting Act 1990. One of its roles is to regulate programmes and advertising on independent radio.

Licensees (that is, radio stations) are charged with complying with the Code. This means that they must ensure that the advertising and sponsorship which they broadcast meets the requirements of the Code. The Radio Authority will give advice to its licensees about the Code's provisions. Advertisers should liaise with the radio stations about specific advertisements rather than approach the Radio Authority direct. The Radio Authority investigates complaints made under the Codes and publishes details of its decisions in regular reports. An adverse decision is likely to generate adverse publicity for the advertiser. It will also mean that the advertisement must be withdrawn unless it is amended to ensure compliance with the Code. An advertiser who breaches the Code may therefore find that its advertising will be denied an outlet on independent radio.

The Radio Authority can impose sanctions against those radio stations (but not the advertisers) which breach the Code, including fines and, in severe cases, the withdrawal of the station's licence.

Categories of advertisements

Certain types of advertising must be pre-cleared before broadcast by the Radio Advertising Clearance Centre (RACC). The RACC is a separate body to the Radio Authority. The advertisements which *must* be cleared by the RACC are as follows:

(a) advertisements which will appear across the UK;

(b) advertisements for betting and gaming in so far as such advertisements are permitted at all (see below);

(c) commercial services offering advice on personal, consumer or medical problems in so far as such advertisements are permitted at all (see below);

(d) advertisers of, or advertisements concerning matters of, political, industrial and public controversy in so far as such advertisements are permitted at all (see below);

(e) advertisements directed specifically at children and/or containing child voice-overs;

(f) advertisements containing environmental benefits for the products/services being advertised;

(g) advertisements containing testimonials;

(h) advertisements for alcoholic drink;

(i) advertisements for charities;

(j) advertisements for cigars and pipe tobacco;

(k) advertisements for or featuring consumer credit, investment and complex financial advertising;

(l) advertisements making food and nutrition claims;

(m) advertisements for matrimonial, introduction and dating services;

(n) advertisements for medicines, treatments and health;

(o) advertisements for 18-certificate films and videos;

(p) religious advertisers.

Local advertisements not falling within the above categories can be cleared for broadcast by the individual stations concerned. Each station will operate its own clearance procedures. Whether advertisements are cleared by the RACC or the stations themselves, it is advisable that material is submitted for approval at the earliest possible stage, so that if the idea behind an advertisement is fundamentally flawed, it can be spotted at the outset.

Clearance by the RACC

Pre-production scripts must be sent to the Radio Authority with the following details:

(a) the name of the script subscriber;

(b) the identity of the advertiser;

(c) the product/brand which is being advertised;

(d) the title of the script;

(e) the length of the script;

(f) the radio station on which the advertisement will be broadcast (if known);

(g) evidence to support factual claims made in the script.

Recorded versions of advertisements need not be submitted to the RACC, although individual radio stations may wish to check them against the RACC-approved scripts.

Clearance by the RACC or the radio station will not guarantee that the advertisement complies with the Code.

Appeals and judicial review

The decisions of the Radio Authority are subject to judicial review by the courts. There is no other right to appeal the decision to the courts. Readers are referred to Chapter 15 for an outline of the judicial review procedure.

The meaning of 'advertisement'

The Code defines 'advertisement' as any item of publicity (other than a sponsor credit) which is broadcast in return for payment or other valuable consideration (for example, in return for services rendered) made to the radio station or which seeks to sell to a listener any product or service.

The Code's basic rules

The specific rules which are set out below should be read in conjunction with the following basic rules:

(a) radio advertising should be legal, decent, honest and truthful;

(b) advertisements must comply in every respect with the law, common or statute, and licensees must make it a condition of acceptance that they do so comply;

(c) the advertising rules are intended to be applied in the spirit as well as the letter.

The Code's specific rules

The rules in the Code which relate to the use of people in advertising and the making of comparisons are described in Chapters 10 and 8 respectively. Other rules contained in the Code are as follows:

Identification

Advertising breaks must be clearly distinguishable from programming.

There must be no risk that listeners will be confused into believing that an advertisement is a programme. Listeners must be able to recognise the message as an advertisement within a short space of time. References to specific programmes in advertisements are not permissible unless the advertisement is for those programmes or has been placed by a programme sponsor.

Prohibited categories of advertisements

Advertisements for products and services set out below are *not* acceptable:

(a) breath testing devices and products which purport to mask the effects of alcohol;

(b) the occult;

(c) betting and gaming (except bingo (other than in Northern Ireland), non-gaming machines and social non-gambling activities offered by organisations or clubs who also hold gaming licences, advertisements for football pools and certain types of lottery). Advertisements for the exemptions to this rule must not be directed at those under 16 nor likely to be of particular appeal to them. In the case of bingo, advertisements should not be directed at, or likely to appeal to, those under 18 and should not feature or encourage reckless playing;

(d) escort agencies and the like;

(e) cigarettes and cigarette tobacco;

(f) commercial services offering advice on personal, consumer or medical problems (except those operated with the approval of the Local Authority or Local Health Authority or other approved authority which are permitted);

(g) firearms and other weaponry;

(h) pornography;

(i) products for the treatment of alcoholism;

(j) hypnosis, hypnotherapy, psychology, psychoanalysis, psychotherapy or psychiatry (unless approved by the Radio Authority);

(k) advertisements for investments in commodities which are not readily realisable for example, futures or other complex investments;

(l) advertisements for the issues of shares and debentures;

(m) advertisements recommending the acquisition or disposal of an investment in a specific company.

Advertisements for acceptable products/services will become unacceptable if they give publicity to an unacceptable product or service.

Presenter-read advertisements

Station presenters may provide voice-overs for commercials (other than those for medicines or treatments) provided they do not endorse, recommend, identify themselves with or personally testify about an advertiser's products/services.

Misleadingness

Advertisements must not contain any descriptions, claims or other material which might, directly or by implication, mislead about the product or service advertised or about its suitability for the purpose recommended. Advertisements must clarify any important limitations or qualifications. Before accepting advertisements, licensees must be satisfied that the advertiser has adequately substantiated any descriptions or claims.

Evidence must therefore be available to support the factual claims in advertisements at an early stage. It should be borne in mind that any implied or indirect claims must be supported whether or not they were intended. Care should be taken to avoid unintentional claims.

The Radio Authority is under a duty pursuant to the Control of Misleading Advertisements Regulations 1988 to investigate complaints about misleading advertisements. The reader is referred to Chapter 7 for an analysis of the provisions of the regulations.

The reader is also referred to the section of Chapter 18 (concerning the ITC Codes) about misleading advertising for a further explanation of the types of advertisement which might mislead.

The practice notes which accompany the Radio Authority Code make allowance for the use of puffery, that is, statements or descriptions that are obviously exaggerated. Such statements will not be misleading if it is obvious that they are not meant to be taken at face value. Where puffery might be seen as factual it must be substantiated. The line between puffery and factual statements is often a difficult one to draw. The practice notes point out that particular care should be taken when making superlative claims, for example, best, cheapest, etc. Unless it is clear that such claims are not meant to be taken seriously, evidence must be produced to support them. Factual claims in sung jingles must be substantiated in the same way as the spoken word.

Political, industrial and public controversy

No advertisement may be broadcast by, or on behalf of, any body whose objects are wholly or mainly of a political nature and no advertisement may be directed at a political end.

The term 'political' has a broader meaning than 'party political'. The type of issues which are classified as 'political' are explored in relation to the ITC Code (see Chapter 18) which contains a similar provision.

No advertisement may have any relation to any industrial dispute (other than an advertisement of a public service nature inserted by, or on behalf of, a government department). An advertisement may not show partiality in matters of political or industrial controversy or relating to current public policy.

Taste and offence

Advertisements must not offend against good taste or decency or be offensive to public feeling.

The Code recognises that standards of taste are subjective. Radio stations are required to exercise responsible judgments taking into account the sensitivities of all sections of their audience when deciding on the acceptability of advertising and its scheduling.

The practice notes set out guidance for avoiding causing offence in advertising. They suggest that the following should be avoided:

(a) unkind or hurtful references to minority groups;

(b) deprecating or hurtful references to religious or political beliefs;

(c) demeaning comments or comments which ridicule those suffering from physical or mental difficulties or deformities;

(d) salacious or indecent themes and sexual innuendo likely to cause serious or widespread offence;

(e) sexual stereotyping likely to cause serious or widespread offence;

(f) offensive and profane language.

Care should be taken when advertising material whose contents may offend to ensure that the advertising is not offensive.

The above guidance is not intended to be exhaustive.

Superstitions and appeals to fear

Advertisements must not exploit the superstitious and must not without justifiable reason play on fear.

An example of a justifiable reason might be an advertisement designed to encourage listeners to take steps to improve their welfare, for example, encouraging the fitting of a smoke alarm.

Price claims

Advertisements must comply with the provisions of the Consumer Protection Act 1987. Readers are referred to Chapter 6 for further detail.

Testimonials

The practice notes to the Code define a testimonial as an expression of view or statement of experience of a real person.

Testimonials must be genuine and must not be misleading. Licensees are required to obtain satisfactory documentary evidence in support of any testimonial or claim *before* accepting it for inclusion in an advertisement. Children are not allowed to give testimonials. Celebrities are not permitted to give testimonials about medicines or treatments, although they may provide a voice-over or commentary for such advertisements, provided that what they say does not amount to a testimonial. Station presenters are not permitted to testify on their own station about any products or services which they use.

Fictional playlets involving characters expressing, by way of drama, the views of an advertiser are permitted, but it must be made clear that the situation and people depicted are not real.

Guarantees

Advertisements must not contain the words 'guarantee', 'guaranteed', 'warranty' or 'warranted' or words with similar meanings unless the radio station concerned is satisfied that the terms of the guarantee are available for inspection and are outlined in the advertisement or made available to the purchaser at the point of sale or with the products/services. The terms of a guarantee must set out the remedial action available to the purchaser.

The above does not apply where the word 'guarantee' is used colloquially and would clearly be understood not to refer to the advertiser's offer.

Use of the word 'free'

Advertisements must not describe products or samples as 'free' unless they are supplied at no cost or at no extra cost (other than postage or carriage) to the recipient.

Competitions

Advertisements inviting listeners to take part in competitions are permissible, provided that the competition complies with the Lotteries and Amusements Act 1976 (except in Northern Ireland where the Act does not apply). The reader is referred to Chapter 9 for the requirements of the Act. Licensees have to satisfy themselves that prospective entrants can obtain printed details of a competition, including announcement of results and distribution of prizes, before entry.

Premium rate telephone services

The ICSTIS Code applies to the advertising on radio of premium rate telephone services. The Radio Authority Code particularly refers to the need to include certain information, namely, pricing information, the identity of the service provider and its address (or that of the information provider), a warning about calls which normally last over five minutes and the need for advertisements for live conversation services to state whether conversations are being continuously recorded.

Advertisements should not encourage people under 18 to call live conversation services.

Sexual and racial discrimination

The Code reminds licensees/advertisers that it is illegal for an advertisement to discriminate against women or men in opportunities for employment, education or training and also that it is illegal for an advertisement to discriminate against ethnic minorities. Advertisements must not contain material which might reasonably be construed by ethnic minorities to be hurtful or tasteless.

Sound effects

Advertisements must not include sounds likely to create a safety hazard to drivers, for example, the sound of sirens or children screaming.

Direct marketing, for example, mail order and direct response

The provisions of this rule are detailed and identical to the rule in the ITC Code. Readers are referred to Chapter 18 for further details of the Code's provisions.

The Radio Authority Code contains detailed rules dealing with the following:

(a) financial advertising;

(b) alcoholic drink advertising;

(c) advertising and children;

(d) medicines, treatments and health;

(e) charity advertising;

(f) environmental claims;

(g) religious advertising; and

(h) matrimonial and introduction agencies.

The rules in relation to programme sponsorship

For the purposes of the Code, a programme is sponsored if it is broadcast in return for payment or other valuable consideration to the radio station. Sponsorship of programmes does not have to be cleared in advance by the RACC – even if the programme in question is broadcast nationally.

What programmes can be sponsored?

All programmes can be sponsored with the exception of news *bulletins*, whether local, national or international. 'Bulletin' does not include news features or news magazine type programmes, which may be sponsored with some restrictions (see below).

Who can sponsor?

Certain types of businesses cannot sponsor programmes without prior approval from the Radio Authority. These businesses which are prohibited from advertising (see p 218) may only sponsor programmes with the written approval of the Radio Authority. Religious programmes and features of any description directed particularly at children (those aged 15 and below) must not be sponsored by companies whose commercial interests involve sanitary protection, family planning, contraceptives, pregnancy testing and anti-AIDS or anti-drugs messages.

Religious programmes and features of any description directed particularly at people under 18 must not be sponsored by companies whose commercial interests involve alcohol, cigars or pipe tobacco.

Companies with betting and gaming interests are also subject to certain restrictions, most significantly that they cannot sponsor programmes specifically designed for or aimed at children (those aged 15 and below).

Programme content

The Code permits a direct link between programme content and the commercial activities of the sponsor, for example, a sportswear manufacturer can sponsor a sports programme.

Ultimate editorial control of sponsored programmes belongs to the radio station rather than the sponsor. However, subject to that proviso, sponsors may contribute to the editorial of most programmes, for example by suggesting information, advice and ideas. The programme content must not, however, under any circumstances, contain an endorsement of the sponsor's products or services. A sponsor must not seek to sell its own products within a programme editorial.

Advertising and sponsorship

Sponsors may purchase advertising spots in and around the programme they sponsor. However, care should be taken to ensure that their advertisement would not be confused with the programme (see p 218).

Sponsorship credits

Sponsor funding and contribution to programmes must be clearly acknowledged so that listeners can recognise sponsored programmes and any contribution to editorial content that has been made by sponsors.

Credits must clearly be identified as credits. They must not be liable to be confused with the sponsor's advertisements. They must contain the programme title and/or a description of the programme's subject matter, the name of the sponsor, an expression of the sponsor's contribution to the production of the programme (for example, whether it was financial or editorial) and a brief identification of the sponsor's commercial activities where they are unlikely to be obvious. Any link between the programme's subject matter and the sponsor's commercial activities should also be made clear. Credits can include the sponsor's advertising jingles and slogans or brand and corporate names, provided that the credits would not be mistaken for an advertisement.

Product placement (that is, the gratuitous mentioning of brand names in programmes) is prohibited.

CHAPTER 20

THE INDEPENDENT COMMITTEE FOR THE SUPERVISION OF STANDARDS OF TELEPHONE INFORMATION SERVICES (ICSTIS)

REGULATION FOR TELEMARKETING

About ICSTIS

The Independent Committee for the Supervision of Standards of Telephone Information Services (ICSTIS) is a body funded by members of the telecommunications industry to set and review standards relating to the content and promotion of premium rate telephone services through the ICSTIS Code of Practice.

Premium rate services are telephone services with an information or entertainment element, which are generally charged for at higher rates than standard telephone calls. The type of services offered on a premium rate basis are varied and range from chat lines, weather services and sports results to marketing services.

Types of marketing services

The range of marketing services which can take place via premium rate services is without limit. It could include, for example, a method of entry into competitions. Contestants could be asked to call a premium rate number with an answer to a question. Consumers can also be given details of a premium rate number to call for details of a company's product range and prices. The use of premium rate services for such activities is growing rapidly.

Industry set up

In order to understand how the ICSTIS Code of Practice operates, it is necessary to appreciate how the premium rate telephone industry operates.

Network operators are the entities which run the telecommunications networks which carry premium rate services. The network operators fund ICSTIS and include bodies such as BT, Mercury Communications and Orange. The network operators will contract with *service providers*, which are the entities which actually provide the premium rate services. Some service providers will provide lines and call handling facilities to businesses which front their own premium rate services.

Part of the cost of a premium rate call is passed by the network operator to the service provider and any other entity involved in providing the service, for example, the business which is using the service for marketing purposes.

The network operators support ICSTIS. As part of their contract with service providers, they will require the providers to comply with the ICSTIS Code of Practice. Those with whom the service providers contract will generally be placed under the same obligation. The interlocking nature of the contractual provisions is intended to oblige compliance with the ICSTIS Code throughout the industry. Responsibility for compliance rests with the service providers, regardless of their responsibility for the content of any particular service. ICSTIS explain that this ensures that Code breaches are not lost in argument between the various parties involved in providing a service about their respective responsibility for the breach.

The functions of ICSTIS

ICSTIS has issued a Code of Practice relating to the content and promotion of premium rate telephone services. There is also a separate ICSTIS Code of Practice regulating live conversation services. ICSTIS monitors services to ensure that they comply with their standards and investigates and adjudicates upon complaints made under the Code.

What happens when complaints are upheld

ICSTIS will recommend measures to achieve compliance with the Code. ICSTIS also has a range of sanctions which it can impose on service providers. These range from the imposition of fines, the barring of access to a service or a number of services or, in severe cases, preventing a company from providing any premium rate services.

A guide to the contents of the Code

The Code applies to all premium rate services which are accessed in the UK, whether those services are provided from the UK or from abroad and whether the service provider is situated in the UK or abroad.

Promotion of premium rate services includes anything where the intent or effect is directly or indirectly to encourage the use of premium rate services.

Services and promotional material for such services must not contain material which is in breach of the law, nor omit anything which the law requires. They must not facilitate or encourage anything which is unlawful.

Services and promotional material for such services must not contain material indicating violence, sadism or cruelty or be of a horrible or a repulsive nature. They must not involve the use of foul language. They must not be of a kind likely to cause grave or widespread offence or debase, degrade or demean. Nor must they result in any unreasonable invasion of privacy, induce an unacceptable sense of fear or anxiety or encourage or incite any person to engage in dangerous practices or to use harmful substances.

Factual claims

Services and promotional material must not be of a kind likely to mislead by inaccuracy, ambiguity, exaggeration, omission or otherwise. Before promoting or providing services, the service provider must have readily available all documentary and other evidence necessary to substantiate factual claims. This material, with a statement explaining its relevance, must be made available to ICSTIS without delay if ICSTIS requests it.

Services must not contain inaccurate information. It should be made clear to callers when time-sensitive data was last updated. In the case of services promoted in publications or other media with a shelf life of three months or more, a statement must be included in the promotion to the effect that the information given is correct at the date of publication and that date must also be stated. If the call charges increase during the life of the promotion, the service must be prefaced with a message informing callers of the new rates.

Service providers must take all reasonable steps to ensure that promotional material does not reach those for whom the service concerned may be inappropriate. The Codes of Advertising and Sales Promotion (considered in Chapter 17) should also be complied with.

Pricing information

The service provider must ensure that the charge for calls is clearly set out in *all* promotions. Prices should be set out in the form of a numerical price per minute, inclusive of VAT, or the total maximum cost to the consumer of the complete message or service. Pricing information must be legible and prominent. It should be written horizontally and presented in a way that does not require close examination. Promotions broadcast on television should contain spoken as well as written pricing information if the maximum call cost can exceed £2. Where it is unlikely that callers will be aware of pricing information, for example, where the customer is unlikely to have seen or heard any promotion containing pricing information, the service provider must place a distinct pricing message at the beginning of the service.

No premium rate service should be promoted as being free or in a way which implies that it is free.

Competitions and other games with prizes

All competitions should have a closing date, except those where there are instant prizewinners. An insufficient number of entries is not a sufficient reason for changing the closing date or withholding prizes. Prizewinners must receive their prizes within 28 days of the closing date, unless a longer period is clearly set out in the promotional material. If there is any subjective assessment in the selection of winning entries, judging must be by at least one person who is independent of the service provider and any intermediaries involved in providing the service.

The chances of winning a prize must not be exaggerated. Service providers must have readily available all documentary and other evidence to substantiate any claims relating to the availability of prizes. Words such as 'win' and 'prize' should not be used in respect of gifts which are offered to every participant.

Competitions which offer an alternative postal entry should not suggest that it is necessary to call the premium rate service in order to take part. Participants who enter the competition by post must have the same chance of winning a prize as those who use the premium rate service.

Promotional material must clearly state any information which is likely to affect the decision to participate in the promotion including the following matters:

(a) the closing date of the competition;

(b) significant terms and conditions, including any restriction on the number of entries or the prizes to be won;

(c) a description of prizes to be won, including the number of major prizes;

(d) any significant eligibility restrictions;

(e) promotional material for competition services which can cost more than £1.00 must clearly show the cost per minute and likely playing time or the full cost of the call and details of how the competition operates and an indication of any tie breakers.

The following additional information must also be available to potential competitors, either in the original promotional material or available separately to anyone sending a prepaid envelope:

(a) how and when prizewinners will be informed;

(b) how prizewinner information may be obtained;

(c) any criteria for judging entries;

(d) any alternative prize that is available;

(e) the details of any intended publicity in connection with prizewinners;

(f) any supplementary rules that will apply.

Competition services aimed at or likely to appeal to persons under 16 must not offer cash or anything which can be readily exchanged for cash as a prize or feature long and complex rules.

Competition services which may cost more than £5.00 must, as soon as possible after the caller has spent £2.50 and after each subsequent £2.50 spent, require an active confirmation that the caller wishes to continue. Failure to provide the correct responses must cause the service to be terminated by forced release.

Sales promotion services

Promotional material for a sales promotion must not be misleading. Particular care should be exercised where the caller has no opportunity to examine goods before taking delivery.

Any factor likely to affect a consumer's decision to participate in the promotion must be made clear before the consumer is committed to a purchase upon which participation depends, and included in promotional material for the promotion. These factors will include:

(a) instructions on how to participate;

(b) the full cost and conditions of participation;

(c) any closing date;

(d) any significant eligibility restrictions;

(e) any limit on the number or amount of promotional products on offer.

Promotional material for the promotion should make clear if participants may become involved in further publicity or advertising, whether connected with the sales promotion or not. Participants' names and addresses should not be used in further publicity without their prior written permission.

If an unexpectedly high level of demand might lead to an inability to supply consumers with the promised goods, contingency plans must be made to supply consumers with alternative goods of equal or greater perceived value.

The above is an account of the rules most likely to affect telemarketing. It is not a complete summary of the ICSTIS Code of Practice. Readers are advised to consult a copy of the Code (available free of charge from ICSTIS) where appropriate.

USEFUL ADDRESSES

Trade Mark Register

Patent Office

25 Southampton Buildings

London

WC2A 1AY

Tel: 0171 438 4724/4701/4702/4704

The Committee of Advertising Practice

2 Torrington Place

London

WC1E 7HW

Tel: 0171 580 5555

Fax: 0171 631 3051

Copy Advice and Help Notes

Tel: 0171 580 4100

Fax: 0171 580 4072

The Advertising Standards Authority

2 Torrington Place

London

WC1E 7HW

Tel: 0171 580 5555

Fax: 0171 631 3051

Internet: http://www.asa.org.uk

The Independent Television Commission

33 Foley Street

London

W1P 7LW

Tel: 0171 255 3000

Fax: 0171 306 7800

Broadcast Advertising Clearance Centre

200 Gray's Inn Road

London

WC1X 8HF

Tel: 0171 843 8265

Fax: 0171 843 8154

Radio Authority

Holbrook House

14 Great Queen Street

London

WC2B 5DG

Tel: 0171 430 2724

Fax: 0171 405 7062

Radio Advertising Clearance Centre

46 Westbourne Grove

London

W2 5SH

Tel: 0171 727 2646

Fax: 0171 229 0352

ICSTIS

Alton House

177 High Holborn

London

WC1V 7AA

Tel: 0171 240 5511

Fax: 0171 379 4611

Addleshaw Booth & Co

100 Barbirolli Square

Manchester

M2 3AB

Tel: 0161 934 6000

Fax: 0161 934 6060

and

Sovereign House

PO Box 8

Sovereign Street

Leeds

LS1 1HQ

Tel: 0113 209 2000

Fax: 0113 209 2060

INDEX